DEVELOPING WRITING THROUG

BY MATHEW SULLIVAN

PUBLISHED BY: Creative Educational Press Ltd
2 The Walled Garden
Grange Park Drive
Biddulph
Staffs
ST8 7TA

Tel: 07789938923
Fax: 01782 379398

PRINTED BY: York Publishing Services Ltd.,
64, Hallfield Road, Layerthorpe, York, YO31 7ZQ

ILLUSTRATIONS BY: KL Kwan   gettraught@rocketmail.com
Ian Crowford   musomic@gmail.com

DESIGN: Simon Matthews

PROOFREADING: Angela Burt

Alan Peat   www.alanpeat.com
info@alanpeat.com

Mathew Sullivan   www.inspiredminds.eu
inspiredminds123@gmail.com

Simon Matthews   www.s2air.co.uk
info@s2air.co.uk

ISBN: 9780957079694

Also available from Creative Educational Press Ltd (www.thecepress.com):

Writing Exciting Sentences: Age 7 Plus by Alan Peat
A Second Book of Eciting Sentences by Alan Peat & Mathew Sullivan
50 Ways to Retell a Story: Cinderella by Alan Peat, Julie Peat and Christopher Storey
Get Your Head Around Punctuation (...and how to teach it!) by Alan Peat
The Elves and The Shoemaker 1897 illustrated by John Harrold
Writing Exciting Ghost Stories: Age 9 Plus: Ghost Story Plot Skeletons by Alan Peat
(co-author Julie Barnfather)
Teaching Outstanding Persuasive Writing by Alan Peat
The Magic Stone by Alan Peat (illustrated by John Harrold)
Word Warriors (CD-ROM Game) design by Simon Matthews
Spelling Bee (CD-ROM Game) design by Simon Matthews

AUTHOR BIO:

Mathew Sullivan is a class teacher and Literacy coordinator from Stockport, working in St. Richard's R.C. Primary School, Manchester. He has provided national CPD training on using comics to enhance Literacy teaching (evaluated as 'superb' and 'inspiring' by attendees). He works as creative and pedagogic consultant for the Manchester Metropolitan University Comic SMART initiative, where his techniques are implemented in high schools across Manchester. Mathew has demonstrated his approach in primary schools and high schools around the North West. He co-wrote 'A Second book of Exciting Sentences' with Alan Peat for Creative Educational Press, is an Ofsted graded 'Outstanding' teacher, and was named Silk 106.9 Teacher of the Year in 2012.

THANKS:

To Alan and Julie Peat, for the opportunity to work with you and write this book. Your faith, guidance and support remain immeasurably important and appreciated.

To Claire Philbin, Lucy Bradley, Andrea Toal, Kathryn Broadbent, Sharon Sesnan and Angela Burt for their valuable contributions.

To Simon Matthews, for his outstanding design work and effort.

To Mum and Dad, for their encouragement and love.

And last but by no means least, thank you to the children of St. Richard's, for being a constant source of inspiration and for making me smile every single day.

Dedicated to Lucy Miles.

FEEDBACK

"Inspiring ideas for engaging lessons. Right down to KS1 and Foundation Stage, comics can be used to enthuse and interest even the most disengaged children. The comic planner allows reluctant writers to be inventive and creative, and ideas like pathetic fallacy are presented in such an easy and intuitive way using comics. Excellent ideas for using comics in the classroom to raise children's enjoyment of writing."
Gaz Needle - St Joseph's R.C. Primary School, Oldham

"Just as Steve Rogers became Captain America after taking the Super Soldier Serum, my Year 5 class have started to become sentence making superheroes after we used Mat's amazing comic-based strategies to develop our writing. Constantly engaged, enthused and excited, both boys and girls have loved developing their language and writing through the use of comic stimuli. These ideas are a weapon, more powerful than Thor's hammer, in the fight to nurture exciting and expressive writing in today's classroom."
Gary Wilson – Heyes Lane Primary School, Altrincham

"In this digital age, where children are exposed to many exciting stimuli, comics are the perfect vibrant, dynamic starting point for both reading and writing learning. They are not only exciting and interesting to pupils, but full of fantastic vocabulary, storylines, writers' tricks and much more. Mathew Sullivan is a treasure trove of terrific trialled and triumphed ideas for using comics, and a 'geekish' expert, to boot!"
Heather Wright – The District CE Primary School, St. Helens

"Using comics in the classroom has not only revealed my inner geek, but has inspired and engaged my class in a wide range of subjects. Whether it is dialogue in Literacy, story planning for Viking sagas or organising and structuring information for reports, the children have been amazed that such a relatable and creative format can entice them into producing such brilliant work whilst having so much fun! Visually stimulating, readily differentiated and extremely on trend, Mat's inspirational comic book techniques have provided me with a timeless resource that I am looking forward to using over and over again!"
Hayley Knowles – Mesne Lea Primary School

"These simple but extremely effective ideas engage even the most reluctant of writers: arming them with skills which are transferable across all genres. Whether you are a comic novice (like myself), or a self-confessed 'comic geek', the methods in this book are easy to implement and have a dramatic impact on children's writing. Superb!"
Andrew Currie – Fulbridge Academy, Peterborough

"A fabulous resource that excites both boys and girls. Mat's techniques should be shared widely and celebrated."
Henry Smith, LendMeYourLiteracy Co-founder

"I have seen first-hand how using comics in the classroom can stimulate, motivate and engage children when writing. Mat has demonstrated how comics can be used to develop characters with depth, create exciting story plots, and develop the use of exciting vocabulary and sentences within stories."
Tanasha Robinson, St. Silas School, Liverpool

CONTENTS

Comics, once ignored or even worse derided, are one of the most profitable stimuli for the teaching of writing, and I am delighted to write this introduction to a book about the positive and profitable use of comics in the classroom.

In *Developing Writing Through Comics*, Mathew Sullivan establishes the undeniable potency of the medium as a key tool for developing writing, yet comics are, sadly, still often tainted with the stigma of frivolity; of superficiality. The idea that comics are simplistic is so outdated as to be laughable - read Will Eisner's 'A Contract With God' (1964) or Art Spiegelman's 'Maus' (1991) or Steven Seagle's 'It's a bird' (2005) - the potential sophistication of the medium is undeniable.

I have read, recently, about the 'trend' of using comics in the classroom and I must say that I strongly object to the use of the word in this context as it implies something short-lived, a fad espoused by educational cool hunters. I strongly believe that the broad sweep of practical ideas which Mathew Sullivan explores in the book will, once and for all, ensure that comics are never again viewed as a 'trend' but rather, as an essential classroom tool.

When comics ARE written about positively the general consensus is that they harness the attention of pupils. The strength of this volume is its exploration of what the teacher does once they have that attention, and Mathew neatly avoids the mistake of limiting the potential of comics to that of a 'way into' reading/writing for the less-able pupil...an intermediate step on the path to 'real' literature. This anachronistic perspective merely demonstrates a lack of knowledge of the genre and an outdated hierarchical mindset. It is the polar opposite of Mathew's pedagogy, which harnesses the potential of comics as vehicles for the exploration of complex aspects of narrative, without disregarding the basics!

Mathew does not just deal with the more obvious ways that comics can be used to develop story writing, but also with more sophisticated aspects such as mood development, the mechanics of dialogue and inference. Comics are a powerful teaching tool for children of ALL abilities and the ideas included in this publication won't just motivate pupils, they'll help them to develop into thoughtful writers.

Thankfully there is no 'tick list' of strategies in this book, just a well-written, practical menu-of-possibilities shared by an author who is steeped in the subject. This enthusiasm shines through in the writing and as a result I trust that many more teachers will now incorporate comics into their lessons - the benefits are obvious.

And if you aren't using comics? By Odin's beard you should be!

CHAPTER 1
DEVELOPING WRITING THROUGH COMICS
AN INTRODUCTION

AIMS OF THE BOOK

Developing Writing Through Comics is the culmination of four years spent developing a wealth of practical, accessible and engaging ways to use comics in the classroom. All of the ideas in this book are tried and tested, and have helped raise literacy standards and engagement in primary schools and high schools across the country. Many have also been used in Ofsted-observed lessons, which were judged 'Outstanding'. Most importantly, they have been used to inspire a love of reading and writing in pupils.

The intention of this book is to make the medium of comics accessible to all teachers, and to demonstrate how comics, comic characters and comic-based resources can be integrated into existing literacy approaches in order to increase both enthusiasm for learning and standards in literacy.

WHY COMICS?
DISPELLING COMIC MYTHS

Perhaps the more apt question would be, 'Why not comics?' Why not the one written medium that children read voluntarily? Eagerly? That lights their fire and makes them excited about reading from the moment they pick one up? Well, there's a few presumptions or misgivings surrounding comics that, due to their prevalence, restrict many children's access to this fantastic medium to 'out-of-school only'. Unfortunately, it also means that, as educators, many of us miss out on the opportunity to use this amazing resource as a tool to unlock the potential of the budding writers in our care.

The presumptions? Well, there's that archaic, obstinate perspective that is unfortunately still rearing its head, the one that sees comics as 'low-brow', juvenile, little more than glorified picture books. Devotees to this view would have you believe that comics have no place in school, and that their use is another indicator of pandering to children and dumbing down to appeal to the lowest common denominator. The problem with this view is that it is held by people who haven't actually picked up a comic since they were a child, if at all. I picked up a comic recently, just one I had lying around. In just 26 pages of *Superman Unchained #5*, I picked out the following vocabulary:

Compared to most books found in primary schools, the terminology used in this £2.99, 26-page comic, is markedly more advanced, and this is not a one-off. This is what comics are really like. When coupled with the incredible artwork which explores perspective drawing and sequential illustration, the fact that this medium could be considered 'low-brow' is laughable. We need a 'no-brow' approach – if it enthuses pupils and we recognise its pedagogical potential, it should be used. Put this comic into any class library in the country, and watch pupils scramble to read it. And when they come to one of these words that they don't understand, rather than giving up on it or glossing over it, watch them throw their hand up and ask – because they **want** to know. They care about these characters, and as educators we should recognise and harness that passionate interest.

The fact that some teachers do not make use of pupils' interest in comics actually hints at another potential, much more understandable 'Why not comics?' answer. It is the idea that, to use comics in the classroom, you have to be a comic geek yourself. This is simply not true. Actually, the majority of teachers know more about comics than they think they do! The reason for this is simple – comics are everywhere. They have not been more pervasive and present in popular culture at any time than they are right now. At the time of writing, three comic-based films sit in the list of top ten grossing films *of all time*. *The Dark Knight Rises* and *Iron Man 3* have earned a combined total of just under 2.3 *billion* dollars, while *Marvel's The Avengers* is outstripped only by *Avatar* and *Titanic*. This global interest would not exist if these characters and their stories were inaccessible to all but the geekiest nerd. These heroes, the values they represent, the adventures they go on, and the excitement they inspire, are rooted in the best and oldest traditions of storytelling. Now, the chances are you have seen at least one of these films. Maybe you have seen all of them. Maybe you have every Avengers film on Blu-ray and a Captain America suit hanging in your wardrobe, (just me?) but the point is, even if your only exposure to comics was Adam West in *Batman* on Sunday morning TV – you probably know more than you think you know, because comics are part of our culture. Ask yourself these questions:

> What is Batman's real name?
> What is his sidekick called?
> What is Superman's weakness?
> How did Spider-man get his powers?
> Why might you not want to shake Wolverine's hand?

Without even picking up a comic, chances are you know the answer to most, if not all of these questions. With that in mind, think about what a quick flick through a 26-page comic might tell you. Or a five minute Wiki-search on a character that you know your class loves because half the pupils have lunchboxes with that character plastered all over them! Comics are one of the most accessible, yet least used mediums in the classroom. If this is because teachers think they lack the 'comic knowledge' necessary, it's time to change that misconception.

The last answer to 'Why not comics?' is perhaps the most worrying one. It's an opinion that is even more dangerous and damaging than the 'dumbing-down' idea, and it is that 'comics are for boys – girls won't be interested'. In this book, and when I present on CPD training courses, I share plenty of examples of pupils' writing based on comics to show that my ideas work. Over 70% of these examples are written by girls. Girls love comics. Unsurprisingly, the engaging, timeless characters, the suspenseful action and the emotional journeys all appeal just as much to girls as to boys. That is until some backwards thinking stick-in-the-mud comes along and suggests, "comics are for boys and, anyway, they should be reading 'proper' books". The suggestion that girls don't find comics as interesting as boys do is, to me, blatantly sexist and igno-rant. Thankfully, when I share this sentiment at conferences with 100 teachers or more, there are nods from male and female teachers alike. Again, a no-brow approach is needed – whatever works and engages the children, we should be making the most of it.

So, 'Why comics?' Because so many children love comics. It's a no brainer. Because comics are everywhere, and we all know more than we think we do. Because comics span all ages, genders, ethnicities and intellects. Because their appeal is universal, their content inspirational, and their worth as educational tools absolutely immeas-urable.

That's why.

FINDING YOUR WAY AROUND
HOW TO NAVIGATE THE BOOK

The ideas and activities in this book have been separated into the following six areas:

> Motivating reluctant readers and improving comprehension through comics and comic hybrids (Chapter 2)

> Developing plot and story structure through comics (Chapter 3)

> Developing characterisation through comics (Chapter 4)

> Developing locational writing through comics (Chapter 5)

> Developing punctuation, grammar, vocabulary and spelling through comics (Chapter 6)

> Using comics as a medium for exploring complex narrative themes (Chapter 7).

Within these sections, each activity has a chapter reference, a title, and a summary of the objective of the activity, which you can use to find activities which suit your target skills. For example, if you were looking to develop the use of figurative language in setting descriptions, you might look at Chapter 5 (Developing locational writing through comics) where you would find the following:

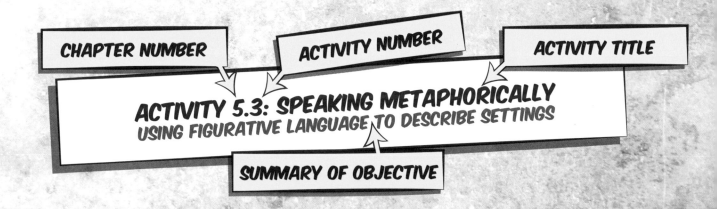

CHAPTER NUMBER

ACTIVITY NUMBER

ACTIVITY TITLE

ACTIVITY 5.3: SPEAKING METAPHORICALLY
USING FIGURATIVE LANGUAGE TO DESCRIBE SETTINGS

SUMMARY OF OBJECTIVE

GETTING STUCK IN
INTEGRATING COMIC-BASED TECHNIQUES INTO PLANNING, TEACHING AND LEARNING

One question I am often asked is, how would one plan for the activities in this book, and do teachers have to chuck out their planning and teach whole units on comics? The answer to that is simple: even I don't teach entire units on comics! Comics are, like any other classroom resource, something to be used where and when appropriate. During the time I have been using comics in literacy I have found the most effective way to integrate them is at the start of a blocked unit. During the planning phase, I will have identified two or three key skills that I know pupils will need in order to write an effective example of whatever text-type it is that we are taking on. These could be, for example, the ability to write an effective opener, to write a flashback, to mix direct and indirect speech, to write from a journalistic perspective, to plan a tale with a moral, to write sequential instructions, and so on. Once identified, I look for opportunities to use a comic stimulus through which I can introduce these target skills in an exciting, engaging way. That is where this book comes in. By identifying the activities that link to your target skills, you can plan and teach these skills through the engaging medium of comics. However, the progression of activities in the book has been designed so that, by the end of the sequence, pupils will have moved away from the comic stimulus and will be applying the skills learned to whichever target genre that you are studying, while retaining the excitement and engagement generated by the initial comic stimulus.

MEET THE TEAM!
GETTING TO KNOW YOUR SUPERHERO SQUAD

When writing this book we wanted teachers to be able to draw not only from existing comic characters, but to have a cast of new and exciting characters which were tailored to the activities and skills for all the target areas of literacy. And so... our team of talented artists came up with this crew of fantastic individuals!

DARKSPECTRE

STARCOMET

SABERWOLF

MAJOR BRITANNIA

ROBORG

STRIKEBACK

LIGHTNING LAD

THE STELLAR WARRIOR

15

MAXIMILLION VENGEANCE

MAX HITZIG

THE ENFORCER

MAGMAMAN

STITCHFACE

CHAPTER 2
MOTIVATING RELUCTANT READERS AND IMPROVING COMPREHENSION THROUGH COMICS AND COMIC HYBRIDS

COMICS AND COMIC HYBRIDS AS TOOLS TO MOTIVATE RELUCTANT LEARNERS

In November 1971 a forward-thinking 33-year-old teacher by the name of W. John Schiffermuller wrote his first letter to a comic magazine, Marvel Comics' The Avengers #93. Here is a little of what he had to say;

"I, as a high school teacher, use Marvel Comics to generate creative writing assignments, to analyze the elements of a folk hero and a tall tale in my English classes...and to just plain ENJOY.

Tough to get today's teenagers to read???? NOT A BIT!! Sure, many of today's teenagers test out at reading levels as much as six years BEHIND their current grade. But the cause is often not the students' lack of interest or ability, nor the much-maligned school system's lack of know-how. Often it is simply that the literature their parents were made to digest (and which often gave mental indigestion) just doesn't turn today's kids on.

The by-word for today's youth is...creativity! ...with the visual boost of Marvel Comics to enlarge the concepts of visualisation...even today's 'tuned-out, turned-off teen-freaks', as one of our legislators called them in a speech, can be stimulated, excited, and...yes, even motivated!"

Over 40 years ago Mr Schiffermuller summed up some of the key reasons why comics belong in the classroom, including their versatility as a medium for inspiring and improving writing as well as engaging reluctant readers. In a televised interview twenty years later, comic giants Stan Lee (co-creator of Spider-man, Iron Man and The Fantastic Four, to name but a few) and Will Eisner (greatly influential in establishing the graphic novel form) also discussed the place of comics in education:

Will Eisner: Teachers have been frustrated by the reluctance of children to read, and so they are reaching out for anything they can get their hands on.

This medium...is now probably the most proliferating literary form in this country. It is the new literacy.

Stan Lee: It's also one of the greatest weapons against illiteracy, because comics are the only things today that a youngster will read voluntarily, nay, eagerly, and obviously the more a kid reads, the more they develop a facility at reading.

Once again, more than twenty years ago, we find individuals promoting the use of comics in the classroom as a key tool for improving literacy skills. Thankfully, that torch is still carried by many, one of whom is the successful children's author Guy Bass. His Atomic! series deals with the day-to-day lives of two superhero children. This chapter will demonstrate how the first Atomic! book, The Vengeance of Vinister Vile, (being a comic/novel hybrid) can be used as the perfect platform for engaging reluctant readers.

When asked if he ever wanted to be a superhero when he was younger, Guy said: "That was all I wanted to be...Superman, Tarzan, The Hulk, Spider-man – they were my heroes growing up. As soon as I could walk I wished I could fly. As soon as I could write and draw I was making up my own superheroes."

It is not difficult to see where the inspiration for Atomic! lies; the book revolves around the characters Jonny and Tommy Atomic (sons of the celebrated superhero Captain Atomic). They are forced to keep their super powers 'under wraps' and attend 'normal school'. The book is also unique, and perfect for our comic-based purposes, because it shifts from novel to comic form and back again throughout.

GUY BASS

ATOMIC!

THE VENGEANCE OF VINISTER VILE

ACTIVITY 2.1: LET'S GET STARTED
CREATING ENGAGING OPENERS

Begin with a speaking and listening activity that never fails to spark an enthusiastic discussion – ask the children to name their favourite superheroes. Have them explain their choices, including what they particularly admire about the character, and ways in which they would like to be like their chosen hero. This dialogue will generate excitement as well as providing you with an engaging segue into the *Atomic!* text. Ask the pupils, "What links all your chosen characters?" You may have a few suggestions here (possibly all 'good guys,' similar powers, etc) but steer them towards **age**. The probability is that they will all have chosen **adult** superheroes. Point this link out, and then ask the group to consider the idea of a **child** superhero. Ask them, "What if one of you were a superhero, but you couldn't tell anyone? How do you think life would be?" After discussing ideas, reveal that the story that they will share today is based on exactly that idea, the lives of two young, secret, superhero brothers.

METHOD

> Share the opening of *Atomic! The Vengeance of Vinister Vile*:

THE NEAR FUTURE

It was the same day that the 777th Interferion Intergalactic Invasion Fleet invaded Earth. Fortunately, their entire space fleet was smaller than a grain of sand, so no one noticed.

It was also the day that Earth's 856th superhero put on his costume for the very first time. He called himself The Flaming Piglet. (He was neither.)

And it was the day that supervillain and all-round bad egg Vinister Vile attacked Albion City for the nineteenth time.

> Discuss what makes this opener effective. If the pupils don't 'spot it', discuss the fact that the balance of humour and mystery draws the reader in. Whilst the idea of a seemingly grand alien invasion falling flat owing to its miniscule size is funny and engaging, the reader will also want to know more about them, and more about what happened on that day. The humorous idea of an inappropriately named superhero makes us laugh, but simultaneously informing the reader that there are 855 other superheroes in the *Atomic!* world makes them wonder who these heroes are and what they might be like. Finally, the introduction of Vinister Vile, and the revelation that this is his nineteenth attack, makes the reader ask the question, "What happened the last eighteen times, and who stopped him?"

> Using this idea of balancing humour and mystery to open a story and draw a reader in, challenge the group to come up with statements that could be substituted for this text. Model some examples and compile some as a group to support writing:

It was the same day that Captain Lightning and The Fizzer finally had a race, London to Australia and back again. They were so fast they completed the contest before anyone had realised they'd set off, so no one believed them and they were both declared loser liars with their pants on fire.

It was the same day Captain Cliché embarked on his journey to steal all the tea in China, all the frogs in France, and all the rain in Spain. He was promptly caught by Old Bill and learned that all that glistens was indeed not gold.

It was the same day that Mr Maniac came up with the idea for an "ultra-devastating, world-ending, staff-of-woe-and-destruction!" Fortunately he didn't have the first clue how to build this staff, but he was very pleased with the name all the same.

> Discuss the structure of these statements (opening with a heroic or dastardly sounding occurrence, then undercutting it, whilst leaving the reader with a question), then challenge the children to follow the examples and make up their own. As well as helping to extend their vocabulary and encouraging them to think about structuring complementary sentences, this introductory exercise will open up the *Atomic!* world. It is a world filled with flamboyant superheroes and villains, some amazing, some inept, some completely ridiculous, but all useful in terms of hooking a reader's interest and crafting an engaging narrative.

ACTIVITY 2.2: IS IT A NOVEL? IS IT A COMIC? NO, IT'S ATOMIC!
CONVERTING VISUAL NARRATIVES

Once you have started reading *Atomic!* it doesn't take long for the book to reveal a key method for engaging reluctant readers. On page 12, during a heated exchange between the two super-brothers Jonny and Tommy (regarding whether they should strive to be 'ordinary' or not), the book changes from a written narrative to a comic.

This switch provides us with a gateway to improving literacy through the less threatening, more subjective approach of 'visual literacy'. The idea of 'reading a picture' is much less intimidating to many reluctant or disengaged readers than a page full of printed text. However, it allows a similarly detailed narrative interaction, and provides us with a stimulus that can inspire detailed written projects.

METHOD

> Continue reading the story and focus on page 12 as a group. Open a discussion by asking why the writer felt that this scene, in particular, would be better presented to the reader as a comic rather than a written story. Agree that the physical action in the scene lends itself well to exciting illustrations, but that as a group, using our exciting writing techniques, we could work together to describe what we see just as well in written form.

> Focus on the first cell and show the following simple description:

"Can ordinary people do THIS?" Tommy said. He used his mind powers to push Jonny towards the balcony.

"Heey," Jonny said. He was scared.

> Remind pupils of the editing skills they have developed by displaying and discussing the following expanded description:

"Can ordinary people do THIS?" Tommy exclaimed mockingly as he used his formidable, destructive mind powers to sweep Jonny swiftly off the floor and hurl him forcefully towards the high balcony. Jonny protested, eyes open wide, but it was no use. He was going down.

> Ask the pupils to use what they have learned to identify the effective phrase types and techniques in this description:

RED: Direct speech, correctly punctuated.

YELLOW: Exciting speaking verb.

GREEN: Speaking adverb to add mood.

LIGHT BLUE: Adjective list separated by a comma.

PURPLE: Engaging verb.

NAVY BLUE: Adverb to add intent.

ORANGE: Indirect speech.

PINK: Show not tell.

BROWN: Short sentences for dramatic effect.

KEY

> After reminding pupils of the editing techniques, focus on the second cell and provide them with the following, substandard description:

> "Yaaaahh!" Jonny said. He fell over the balcony. He flew through the air towards the floor below.

> Use the **editing key** to hint at possible improvements to this description:

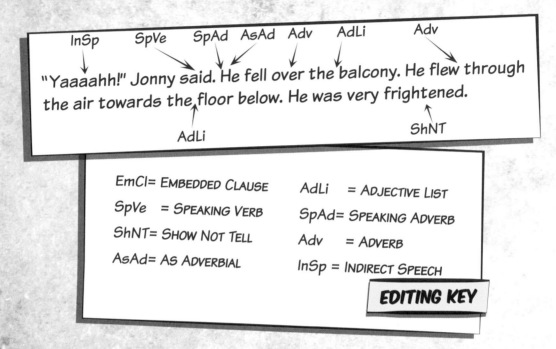

> Model the changed example step by step if necessary, allowing as many suggestions to come from the group as possible:

> Jonny let out an ear-splitting scream. "Yaaaahh!" he bellowed loudly as he toppled head first over the tall, gleaming balcony. Flying frantically through the air, fear choked his scream into a gasp as he curled into a ball and braced for impact...

> Finally, focus on the third cell. Use the following bland description and encourage pupils to select and employ the techniques they have practised, combining them with details they find when 'reading the picture' in order to create an effective description:

> Jonny hit the table with a thud. He bounced off and landed on the floor, making a loud noise.

> Increase independence by reducing support, or, if you think the group is ready, ask the pupils to draw their own three-panelled follow-up, then convert the cells to written descriptions using the practised techniques. By doing this they will have used the less daunting process of 'visual literacy' to improve their comprehension, inference-making and written work.

ACTIVITY 2.3: WHAT HAPPENS NEXT?
CONTINUATION OF NARRATIVE

The illustrated clash between Jonny and Tommy in Activity 2.2 sets the tone for the rest of the book. Jonny wants to live a normal life without the pressure of superhero existence, whereas Tommy strives to embrace his powers and feels stifled by the 'normal' life he is forced to lead. As you read on, taking the occasional opportunity to 'stop-short' can provide the chance for pupils to reflect on what they have learned about the characters. This might then lead to a consideration of what they could infer about how the character's traits and actions may affect and inform future narrative events.

METHOD

> Share with the group the following extract that details part of a day at Babblebrook School:

> "Something else we've got in common. I haven't seen my dad in ages," said Jonny. He held up the picture. "What do you reckon?"
>
> "I dunno – needs something else," Vernon muttered. Jonny rolled up a piece of red paper and stuck it on the picture.
>
> "If in doubt, add more explosions," he said.
>
> "Definitely," giggled Vernon.
>
> In the end, it was a satisfyingly ordinary afternoon all round.
> That is, until the scream.

Looking closely at this extract, we find Jonny and his new friend, Vernon Vincent, enjoying the normality of a fairly mundane art lesson, when all of a sudden the peace and tranquillity is shattered by a scream. Halting at this captivating point provides us with the opportunity to check the children's comprehension before challenging them to use information from the text, including character knowledge, to infer the cause of the scream.

> Point out that whilst Jonny seems happy to have found someone he can relate to within the settled, calm classroom, Tommy is noticeably absent from the scene. We know he does not like the idea of having to be 'normal', he doesn't want to be in school, and he certainly doesn't like hiding his powers, so it's safe to assume that he is the cause of the disruption. Ask the pupils to generate as many possible ideas about what Tommy might have done. Model some ideas if necessary and record the group's contributions:

Tommy has flown out of school, taking all the school books with him.

Tommy has tied up the teacher with skipping ropes and is dangling her from the top of a tree.

Tommy has made a giant robot out of the playground climbing frame and is using his telekinetic powers to make it walk around the school.

Tommy has convinced his teacher that there is a ghost in the room as he controls a piece of chalk and writes a scary message on the board.

Tommy has created a force-field bubble around his teacher and she is stuck to the spot.

> Once you have collected a useful number of suggestions, extend this activity by combining/linking some ideas;

Tommy has tied up the teacher with skipping ropes and has also made a giant robot out of the playground climbing frame. He is using his telekinetic powers to make it walk around the school, carrying the trussed-up teacher as it goes.

> Using the end of the original text as a starting point and applying the techniques practised in *Activity 2.2*, challenge the pupils to expand upon their plot suggestions to write their own versions of the ensuing section of the narrative:

In the end, it was a satisfyingly ordinary afternoon all round. That is, until the scream.

Jonny knew instantly that this had to be Tommy's doing. He couldn't possibly keep his selfish, boastful ways to himself for a whole day. Quickly, (but not so quickly that he revealed his super speed,) Jonny clambered to the nearest window. His mouth dropped. His eyes widened so far his eyeballs almost fell out. His fingers gripped the old, wooden windowsill tight enough to crack it, but thankfully no one noticed. They were all distracted by the unbelievable sight of what seemed to be a very hastily-put-together, gigantic, angry, metal robot, carrying a large, screaming sack, headed straight towards the school.

"Sacks don't scream!" Vernon announced in alarm, as Jonny suddenly realised exactly what was dangling from the deformed giant's arm.

"Oh no he didn't!" Jonny pleaded to himself, but he knew all too well what the sack really was. As the giant moved closer, he could see a plume of blue hair sticking out of the top of the parcel. It was Ms Crackdown, all trussed up, head to toe, with skipping rope. There was only one person capable of such super-powered mischief...

Giving pupils the chance to continue a given narrative means that they can combine their text comprehension skills with writing techniques learned in earlier comics-based lessons. Reluctant writers will enjoy the support of the provided story starter and a familiar, motivating writing context. By halting at a given point during the reading of an engaging text, we are ensuring maximum engagement. We can subsequently encourage pupils to think critically about what they have read, using what they know to inform empathetic, inference-based writing in a context that boosts their writing confidence.

USING COMIC HYBRIDS TO IMPROVE COMPREHENSION

Reading reluctance has many different causes. Perhaps the most readily combatable of these is a lack of motivation. As adults we realise that sometimes we have to do things we don't necessarily care for, or enjoy. Some children may not be mature enough to grasp this, and as such, levels of effort are often matched by level of engagement; a pupil's lack of inclination to develop reading and comprehension skills through uninspiring texts shouldn't really surprise us.

A possible solution? Comics in the classroom! Ensuring that the stimulus is as *engaging*, *relatable* and *enjoyable* as possible, so that a positive cycle of engagement occurs:

Exciting, engaging and relatable texts

Increased reader excitement and enjoyment

Reader develops a more positive attitude to reading and actively seeks to read more

The provision of an exciting, relevant stimulus, such as comics, can result in a near-instant increase in enjoyment and engagement.

Increased reader focus and effort

Reader enjoys new found confidence and improved results

Improved reading skills, comprehension and results

In this chapter, thus far, we have considered how the exciting, relevant stimulus of *Atomic!* can be used to engage reluctant readers and draw them into critical thinking and written work through their enthusiasm for superheroes. We will now consider how the text can be used to develop more traditional comprehension skills, without detracting from the established level of engagement, in order to continue on the cycle of increased positive learning attitude.

ACTIVITY 2.4: CRACKDOWN COMPREHENSION
USING A FAMILIAR SCENE TO IMPROVE CLOSE READING SKILLS

By now, the children will know the basics of the *Atomic!* story: two superhero brothers are struggling to adjust to their new, 'normal' lives. Tommy Atomic despises school, for one reason in particular – his teacher, Ms Crackdown. In this activity we will consider how to improve comprehension skills by examining the scene which details Jonny and Tommy's first day in their new class with this teacher, a scene that the children will all be familiar with (ensuring relevance and engagement). It will also allow you to look fantastic in comparison, and you will most likely relish the opportunity to ham it up as Ms Crackdown in order to make the scene live for the children!

METHOD

> Share the following scene – remember to overact – be evil!

"That is Sir Percival," continued Ms Crackdown, her voice softening slightly. "I named my car because lifeless objects are reliable and trustworthy. Children, however, are ticking time bombs of expectation and high hopes, and must be reminded of their failings at all costs."

"I want to go home," whispered a terrified Vernon as he sat down.

"Thank you, Four-eyes. You just reminded me of rule FOUR!" Ms Crackdown barked. "If you wish to speak, raise your hand. I will then decide whether you deserve my attention, which you probably won't."

Tommy raised his hand. Ms Crackdown stared at him.

"Yes?" she snapped.

"Is it too late to join another class?" asked Tommy.

"Tommy...!" whispered Jonny.

Ms Crackdown took a deep, whistling breath through her nostrils.

"A willful creature, are you?" she said, finally. "Well, we'll soon change that."

She took out a stack of papers and began handing them around the class. "Now, because it is the first day of term – and to ensure that any lingering memories of your oh-so-happy, Mummy-and-Daddy-took-me-to-the-beach-and-bought-me-an-ice-cream summer holidays are wiped from your minds – I have prepared a test for you. Not for any good reason, but because I can. You have ten minutes. If you do not pass, I will personally call your parents and tell them how lazy, stupid and ugly you are."

There was a stifled groan as Ms Crackdown handed out the last test paper with a "Well, don't just gawp at it, woodlice – begin."

> Having shared the text, discuss what the children think of Ms Crackdown. If you are brave enough, stay in character while delivering the working instructions! They can use the same text to work on three areas of comprehension:

1. BASIC COMPREHENSION — FACT FINDING

2. BASIC INFERENTIAL UNDERSTANDING AND WORD-LEVEL WORK

3. INDEPENDENT WRITING WORK BASED ON THE TEXT

AREA 1: BASIC COMPREHENSION — FACT-FINDING

Use the questions below to help pupils practise 'fact-finding'. Discuss techniques like skimming the text (deciding where they should look first), and identifying key words to aid their search.

Use this first question and guide to discuss the skills necessary for accurate fact-finding:

Q1. What does Ms Crackdown call her car?

Guide: Look for **key words** and terms. **Ms Crackdown** is a key term; it lets us know which character we need to focus on. **Call** is a key word, it means we are probably looking for speech, and we are definitely looking for a name. **Car** is a key word; we are looking for where Ms Crackdown makes reference to her vehicle. Using these keywords, identify the exact phrase in the text which contains the answer:

"That is Sir Percival," continued **Ms Crackdown**, her voice softening slightly. "I **named** my **car** because lifeless objects are reliable and trustworthy.

Having successfully located the information, we need to format it into a clear, accurate response. This is where the question actually comes in handy. Take the end of the question:

...Ms Crackdown call her car?

Change the wording slightly:

Ms Crackdown calls her car

Then add the information you have found:

Ms Crackdown calls her car Sir Percival.

These steps may seem obvious, but involving pupils in the process of identifying key words and phrases; using them to scan and home in on the relevant information, and then enabling them to format that information into a clear and accurate answer will facilitate their ability to tackle any fact-finding question, regardless of the source material. Have them practise the process on a selection of the following questions:

Q2. Why did Ms Crackdown give the children a test?

Q3. How many rules are there in Ms Crackdown's classroom?

Q4. What will Ms Crackdown do if someone does not pass her test?

Q5. What does Ms Crackdown call the children?

Q6. What does Vernon want?

Q7. What are children, as far as Ms Crackdown is concerned?

Q8. What happens to Ms Crackdown's voice when she talks about Sir Percival?

Q9. How long do the children have to complete the test?

Q10. What does Ms Crackdown call Vernon?

AREA 2: BASIC INFERENCE-MAKING AND WORD-LEVEL WORK

After establishing the essential fact-finding skills, pupils can tackle inference-based questions. These will necessitate a combination of the method learned and practised in Area 1, with the empathetic skills that were introduced in the character development chapter, as well as some critical thinking. Again, using the following example question and the subsequent guide, explain and model an effective approach to these more complex questions:

Q1. Why does Vernon whisper when he speaks?

Guide: Look for **key words and terms**. In this example, **Vernon** is a key term; it lets us know which character we need to look out for. **Whisper** is a key word; it means we are looking for an example of quietened speech, and it may also be the exact speaking verb we need to find. **Why** is perhaps the most crucial key word; we are being asked to provide a **reason** for a character's actions. For us to be able to do that, we must identify the exact phrase in the text that contains the dialogue, read around it, and use **empathy** to assume the frame of reference of the character in order to explain their actions:

"I want to go home," whispered a terrified Vernon as he sat down.

Having used the key words to find the important phrase, we can instantly see an emotional adjective: Vernon is terrified. But it is not enough to say that this is why he whispers when we can use empathy to discover what he is **terrified** of. Let's put ourselves in his place. He is in a new class, surrounded by strangers, and there is an awful dragon of a teacher hurling orders at him. He is terrified of his new teacher and doesn't want to get into trouble! We can take and use the question to format a clear and accurate answer. Once again, apply the concluding part of the question in the following manner:

...Vernon whisper when he speaks?

Change the wording slightly:

Vernon whispers when he speaks

Then add the information you have found:

Vernon whispers when he speaks because he is terrified of Ms Crackdown and does not want to get into trouble.

Encourage the pupils to practise this combination of fact-finding, empathy and critical thinking on the following selection of Atomic! based questions:

Q2. Why does Ms Crackdown call the children 'woodlice'?

Q3. What does she mean by 'ticking time bombs'?

Q4. Why do the class 'stifle' their groans?

Q5. Why does Jonny react badly to Tommy's cheeky question?

Q6. Why does Ms Crackdown's voice 'soften' when she talks about Sir Percival?

Q7. What does the name 'Ms Crackdown' suggest about the character?

Q8. What is the effect of linking all the words together in Ms Crackdown's description of the summer holidays?

Q9. Why is it strange that Ms Crackdown adds 'ugly' to the list of things to tell a failing child's parents?

Q10. Why might Ms Crackdown think it is acceptable to call pupils names?

Extend this inference work with the following (similar) questions, this time with a focus on word-level work to aid vocabulary development and grammatical understanding.

Q1. "You just reminded me of rule FOUR!" Ms Crackdown barked.
Circle the word which is closest in meaning to the speaking verb 'barked.'
Murmured   Shouted   Dog   Complained   Asked

Q2. Find and list five effective verbs in the text.

Q3. Ms Crackdown describes Sir Percival as 'reliable and trustworthy.' What does reliable mean?

Q4. 'A willful creature, are you?' she said.
Give four alternative speaking verbs for 'said' that would fit into this sentence.

Q5. "Is it _____ late _____ join the other class?" asked Tommy.
Fill the blanks in this sentence with the correct use of to, two or too.

Q6. Change the dialogue from question 5 into indirect speech.

Q7. "I want to go home," whispered a terrified Vernon as he sat down.
Circle the word which is opposite in meaning to the adjective 'terrified'.
Scared   Unafraid   Terrific   Bored   Distracted

Q8. "I will then decide _____ you deserve my attention, _____ you probably won't."
Fill the blanks in this sentence with the correct use of which or witch and weather or whether.

Q9. "I want to go home," whispered a terrified Vernon as he sat down."
Extend this as adverbial to include another action suitable for Vernon –
whispered a terrified Vernon as he sat down and...

Q10. "Well don't just gawp at it, woodlice – begin."
List 3 alternative words for 'gawp' that would fit in this sentence.

AREA 3: INDEPENDENT WRITING WORK BASED ON THE TEXT

In this final comprehension area, we will combine reading and writing skills learned and practised during previous activities to answer questions which require both a longer response, and a balance of textual reference and personal opinion. On the surface, these types of questions often seem to be asking solely for a pupil's opinion, but in truth they also require supporting evidence from the text – the pupils must provide a substantiated opinion or idea, as opposed to merely offering up their 'gut reaction'. As such, children must know how to find and exploit these evidencing opportunities whilst forming their creative responses.

Use the questions below to discuss and practise the process of formulating written answers that include references to the text. Prompts are given for each, providing clues as to where textual references might be made:

Q1. Imagine you are Ms Crackdown – write the first three rules of your classroom.
We know the fourth rule; try to copy its style. Be like Ms Crackdown; rude, strict and miserable!

Q2. Imagine you are Tommy or Jonny, and Captain Atomic asks you about your day. What would you say?
Tommy hates school so would be negative; he feels like he is better than others and doesn't belong – make sure he sounds judgemental and fed up! He might also say something mean about the 'normal' way Jonny was behaving.

Jonny likes school so would be positive; he would be particularly happy about things that made him feel 'normal.' He might also say something about Tommy's behaviour and lack of self-control; he is worried Tommy might ruin things for him.

Q3. Would Ms Crackdown speak any differently to an adult? Write a short conversation between Ms Crackdown and a pupil's parent after they had failed her test.
We know what Ms Crackdown has threatened to say, make sure that this is part of the conversation. We know how she speaks to children, and she seems an all-round nasty person, so let that come through in the vocabulary and phrases you use.

Q4. How does Tommy feel about Ms Crackdown's test? Write what Tommy does during the test.
Tommy thinks of himself as superior; better than everyone else. Think about how he would want to show that during a test. He also really dislikes Ms Crackdown. Might he do something extra to show that?

Q5. What do you think Vernon thought of Ms Crackdown? Write the conversation he has with Tommy after school.
We know from his talk with Jonny that Vernon doesn't want to be in class, he is terrified and wants to go home. Take this as a starting point and think about how Vernon might feel at the end of the day.
(Relief? Worry about the next day?)

By working through these questions and creating responses that are supported by the text, the pupils will have crafted contextualised writing that demonstrates a balance between imaginative flair and evidenced thinking.

ACTIVITY 2.5: WHAT A PERFORMANCE!
COMPREHENSION FOR WRITING

Having developed comprehension, empathy and contextualised writing skills, we can now introduce a new *Atomic!* stimulus which will enable children to employ and extend these techniques in different genres. This will demonstrate how these transferable skills, strengthened by both the excitement generated by the source material, and the confidence garnered from the positive reader cycle, can be used to improve written work based on any reading context.

METHOD

> Following a near catastrophic coming together between Jonny and Tommy, Vernon is injured and is taken to the Atomic's floating fortress. Share the events that follow with the group:

Vernon pointed at the cylinder of energy. "How does it work?"

"The Core is a clean, perpetual energy source," said Uncle Dogday. "It has been powering the Island for more than forty years, keeping it invisible and keeping it aloft."

"But if something *happened* to it – I mean, if it was damaged?"

"Oh me, oh my, don't panic!" said Aunt Sandwich.

"Quite so, Aunt Sandwich," replied Uncle Dogday, pointing out of a high window into the clear blue sky. "After all, no one out there even knows the Island exists..."

"Vernon, are you OK?" asked Jonny. "You look funny. Is it your head?"

"I'm fine," replied Vernon. He pointed the water pistol at Jonny. "I'm just...sorry."

"Sorry?" repeated a baffled Jonny. "What for?"

"This..."

> Introduce the scene with a selection of comprehension questions, incorporating the range of skills covered so far in this chapter:

Q1. What is the Core?

Q2. What does Vernon point at?

Q3. What is the Core's job?

Q4. Why does Uncle Dogday believe they have no reason to panic?

Q5. Why is Jonny 'baffled'?

Q6. What does Jonny mean when he says "You look funny."?

Q7. What effect does the elipsis mark (...) create in this text?

Q8. "Pointed" or "pointing" is used three times in this text. Give an alternative word.

Q9. Circle the word that is closest in meaning to "Panic."
Calm   Depressed   Worry   Alarm   Sad

Q10. Think about Tommy's character. What would he think of all these questions about the Core and the Base? Write a line of speech for him to go after –
"After all, no one out there even knows the Island exists..."

Q11. Imagine Vernon had pointed the water pistol at Tommy. Use what you know about his character to write a description of his reaction.

> After getting to grips with the scene via the three areas of comprehension, focus on the last exchange between Vernon and Jonny:

"Vernon, are you OK?" asked Jonny. "You look funny. Is it your head?"

"I'm fine," replied Vernon. He pointed the water pistol at Jonny. "I'm just...*sorry.*"

"Sorry?" repeated a baffled Jonny. "What for?"

"This..."

> The end of this dialogue raises the question – **What is "This..."?** – What was Vernon about to do? Instead of reading on to find out, halt and discuss possible continuations with the group based on inferences about the characters, the setting and the action. Note down the most helpful ones (those being the ideas that most effectively balance creativity and substantiated thought). Suggest that you are going to use the class's favourite suggestions to create dramas that reveal what happened next.

> Using one of the effective ideas, discuss how the action might unfold with the class. Show them, using the following example if necessary, how they can use what they know about the characters and the context, as well as **their own ideas**, to create a script for a group drama:

IDEA

Vernon squirts his water gun at Jonny; it turns out to be full of a freezing liquid that sticks Jonny to the spot. Vernon then turns his weapon on the other members of the Atomic squad, freezing them solid. He gets to work on dismantling the Core, just as Tommy gets home...

SCRIPT

Setting: Atomic Island

Characters: Vernon, Jonny, Uncle Dogday, Aunt Sandwich, Tommy

Jonny is showing Vernon around the island. The two of them are speaking to Uncle Dogday and Aunt Sandwich when Vernon pulls out his water pistol and points it at Jonny.

Vernon *(Hesitating)*: I'm just...sorry.

Jonny *(Confused)*: Sorry? What for?

Vernon: This...

(Vernon takes out his water pistol and freezes Jonny to the spot.)

Aunt Sandwich: Oh me, oh my! That Vernon child is positively Vile!

Uncle Dogday: I think you're on to something there! No one freezes an Atomic!

(Uncle Dogday and Aunt Sandwich charge at Vernon, but he freezes them both before they can reach him. Laughing, he heads over to the core.)

Vernon: Fools, it was all so easy! Now to complete my master plan and destroy Atomic Island!

> Challenge the children to complete a full script for the rest of the scene, including any stage directions and emotional hints, properly formatted. Suggest that the most effective scripts will include imaginative, original ideas and will also stay true to the characters and context that the children know from their reading and comprehension activities. Upon completion, check the work against the agreed success criteria to identify the most effective examples, and use those as a basis for small group dramas. This will provide the opportunity to develop empathic skills further by assuming the roles of different characters, which will in turn inform 'genre-switching' writing in the next activities.

USING COMIC HYBRIDS TO EXPLORE A VARIETY OF LITERARY FORMS

We have covered a range of comprehension skills in this chapter, from fact-finding, to empathetic, inference-based, work. Now we will consider how best to use those skills, together with effective writing techniques, to create more elaborate, cross-genre, pieces. We will also link the learning to the chapter on effective planning via the use of the comic medium as a planning tool.

ACTIVITY 2.6:
COMPREHENSION + COMICS = CREATIVE CLARITY

After suffering the wrath of Ms Crackdown for a few days, Tommy decides it is time for revenge. He has lured his horrible teacher to the school swimming pool and has arranged a nasty surprise for her.

METHOD

> Share the following extract with the group, stopping short again at the critical moment:

"No...Look *in* the pool," said Tommy. Ms Crackdown peered into the pool. She could make out a very large, very dark shadow at the bottom. She stepped to the edge of the pool and leaned over to get a closer look. She wondered if it was a bench – that is, until it *moved*. The shape had started to swim to the far end of the pool.

> Halting at this point raises the question, **What was in the pool?** Open up this discussion with the class, sharing ideas and deciding together how each could play-out using what they know about the characters and context from their comprehension work. (i.e. if it is a shark, how did Tommy place it there? How would Ms Crackdown react? What happens next? Etc.)

> Once you have discussed a selection of possible scenarios, tell the group they are going to make their favourite one into a eight-cell comic. Challenge them to plan the comic by writing out the story in just eight sentences, with only one event per sentence (each to go along with one cell of illustration). This time, however, instead of their narrative being a continuation of the story, challenge them to include this focal scene in the middle of their plan, thus necessitating both retrospective and prospective planning. This process will help them think about balancing action over the course of a narrative, as well as planning for plot progression and sequencing events. It will also, as in the planning chapter, provide them with a clear plan for their final piece of writing. Show and discuss an example if necessary:

1. Tommy decides Ms Crackdown is evil and begins to plan a way to bring her down.

2. Tommy leaves the Island early the next morning and visits the zoo, using his mind powers to break into the giant squid tank.

3. Tommy flies to school, carrying the squid with him, eventually leaving it in the pool before heading off to find Ms Crackdown.

4. Ms Crackdown follows Tommy to the pool.

5. Ms Crackdown sees something moving in the deep end.

6. The giant squid bursts out of the pool and grabs Ms Crackdown while Tommy looks on, laughing.

7. From the classroom, Jonny hears the commotion and breaks into the gym to see what's going on.

8. Jonny wrestles the squid off Ms Crackdown and runs away at super-speed, dragging the squid behind him.

> Once the eight-sentence plans are complete, provide the children with the eight-cell planner page (Appendix 3) and ask them to convert their plan into a comic, using one sentence per cell. If necessary, use the following illustrations to show how the first two sentences from the example plan could be turned into comic cells:

1. Tommy decides Ms Crackdown is evil and begins to plan a way to bring her down.

2. Tommy leaves the Island early the next morning and visits the zoo, using his mind powers to break into the giant squid tank.

> Finally, have the children use the finished comics as story planners to create a full written version of their narrative. They can use their effective writing techniques and embed their contextualised writing with character traits discovered through comprehension work. All this whilst following a plan that is clear, structured and fun. If necessary, link teaching back to the first activity in this chapter and use the following example to show how cell one could be converted into a full written narrative:

Planning sentence: **Tommy leaves the island early the next morning and visits the zoo, using his mind powers to break into the giant squid tank.**

Comic cell:

Full narrative:

Tommy felt the hair on the back of his neck bristle with electricity as he prepared to jump from the edge of the massive, floating mass that was Atomic Island. The thin air whistled through his jet black hair and his clothes flapped violently in the wind. 30,000 feet...straight down. No plane. No parachute. No time to lose, he thought. Energetically, Tommy leapt from the island and allowed himself to free-fall through the air. The sensation of the atmosphere tearing at his face and pulling at his eardrums reminded him that he needed to create a force field around himself. Once surrounded and safe, he fixed his eyes on his target.

"LET'S GO!" he yelled determinedly. He felt a surge of energy as he pushed himself downwards, faster and faster, his sights set on Babblebrook Zoo.

> Use the colour-coded skills key to help children identify and explain techniques they might use in their writing.

RED: Direct speech, correctly punctuated.

YELLOW: Exciting speaking verb.

GREEN: Speaking adverb to add mood.

LIGHT BLUE: Adjective list separated by a comma.

PURPLE: Engaging verb.

NAVY BLUE: Adverb to add intent.

ORANGE: Indirect speech.

KEY

PINK: Show not tell.

BROWN: Short sentences for dramatic effect.

41

ACTIVITY 2.7: READ ALL ABOUT IT!
USING COMPREHENSION AND INFERENTIAL SKILLS TO INFORM JOURNALISTIC WRITING

In the previous section we looked at using comprehension and inferential skills to inform script writing. Continue the expansion of writing into a variety of genres by using the headline openers that introduce every *Atomic!* chapter, e.g.

THE ALBION ANNOUNCER

5TH SEPTEMBER

THIRD STRIKE!

Vinister Vile attacks Albion City with a
third monster!
"Now, this is just getting silly,"
say harassed citizens

Much like the 'stopping short' activities that have been suggested previously in this chapter, these titbits of information provide children with just enough detail to spark imaginative discussion, and provide narrative context, without being overly prescriptive or influential.

METHOD

> Consider the headline and subheading with the group and identify questions generated by the information, e.g.

What is the monster like?

What did it do?

What happened the last two times?

What was the result of this attack?

> Use these and any additional questions generated by the group as a basis for an empathic drama activity. Nominate some children to be field reporters going into the Albion City streets just after this event, and others to be the citizens who have witnessed the attack. Challenge the reporters to interview the people, who will respond to their questions either as themselves (imagining themselves in the situation) or as characters they have 'adopted' (e.g. old person, local shopkeeper, police officer, superhero/villain) while the reporter takes notes and quotes.

> After coming together to share the accounts of the attack, ask children to use a combination of the notes and quotes, original information garnered from their comprehension activities, and their own creative input to compile the front page of the Albion Observer, including:

Headline
Modify/extend using word play/puns/alliteration

Subheading
Modify/condense and consider alternative vocabulary

Lead Paragraph
A short summary of the story containing the 5 W's –
Who, What, When, Where and Why

Additional information
Expand on the lead paragraph, perhaps using indirect speech

Eyewitness Accounts
Provide more information and personal, emotional content through direct speech

Follow-up information
Details what has happened as a result of the event and what is predicted for the future

Picture
Photograph capturing a moment of the event or the aftermath

Picture caption
Explains the photograph

> Use the following example, if necessary, to clarify layout and content:

www.albionannouncer.co.uk   www.facetube.com/albionannouncer   @albionannouncer   55p

THE ALBION ANNOUNCER

5TH SEPTEMBER

SINISTER VINISTER UNLEASHES MASSIVE MURDER MONSTER

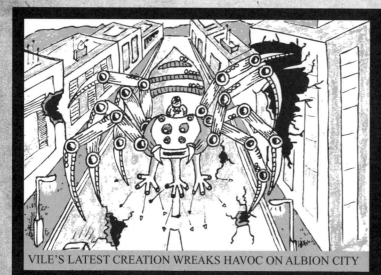

VILE'S LATEST CREATION WREAKS HAVOC ON ALBION CITY

ALBION CITY ATTACKED FOR THE THIRD TIME AS VILE ATTEMPTS TO APPREHEND AND ABOLISH ATOMIC

Vinister Vile, Albion City's most notorious supervillain, let loose yet another terrible creation on the innocent citizens of our fair metropolis yesterday.

The foul fiend unveiled his latest creation on the main High Street at around half one, just as many Albionites were settling into a pleasant afternoon of shopping, drinking tea and gossiping about each other.

Witnesses reported that the mechanical monstrosity had eight legs, rotating guns for fingers, and smelled oddly of elderberries. This is of course quite different to Vile's previous two machines, which have both been flight-capable. Miss Sue Age, who owns the shoe shop on the corner of Bleep Street, speculated on a possible reason for this:

"Well we all know that the last two times Vile has attacked the city, Captain Atomic has destroyed his machines and sent him to jail. His jet pack allowed him to out-manoeuvre Vile's big, heavy monsters. That's why I reckon he went with a land-based murder machine this time. Fat lot of good it did him!"

Mr Rick O'Shea, owner of *Rick's Meats* butchers, was not as optimistic in his view of events. He told the Albion Announcer:

"I'm getting really fed up of being in the middle of all these superhero and supervillain squabbles. Sure, Captain A saved the day again, but this will be the second time I've had to rebuild my shop after some costumed nutcase throws his adversary through my window. The street is covered with my best sirloin

steaks! Someone is going to have to pay for this!"

As the citizens of Albion City start yet another clean-up operation, questions are being asked of the superheroes that they trust to look after them. Can people continue to put their faith in them after the chaos of yesterday? Or is it time to take matters into their own hands? Ben, age 5, of Babblebrook says:

"I believe in heroes like Captain Atomic. My daddy says that as long as he is around, we can all sleep a bit safer at night."

By Phil Graves

HOW DOES CAPTAIN ATOMIC FIT INTO THOSE LYCRA PANTS?

Turn to page 12 to discover his superhero workout secrets

ACTIVITY 2.8:
UNLOCKING THE COMIC POTENTIAL
USING COMICS TO IMPROVE A WIDE RANGE OF LITERACY SKILLS

In this chapter we have looked at how the comic/novel hybrid *Atomic! The Vengeance of Vinister Vile* can be used as a stepping-stone text to engage reluctant learners and improve a range of comprehension skills which we then applied in the pupils' own writing. Although there is a follow-up book, *Atomic! The Madness of Madame Malice*, the truth is that there are very limited numbers of these hybrid texts. In this final activity we will consider the broad range of literacy activities which can be based on just one page of a comic. In this way, once you have finished the *Atomic!* stories, you won't ever be short of learning resources!

METHOD

> Share the following comic page with the group:

> Due to its minimal written content, this page is particularly useful for developing an awareness of visual literacy and for improving inferential understanding. It may, however, be necessary to provide some narrative context:

The Power Squad is a newly formed group of superheroes, one that has come about almost by accident. They work together to fight evil, but they did not join forces by choice. Each member has their own strong personality, their own way of doing things, and believes that they have the right to be leader as they are 'the best'.

Just before this scene, Starcomet was trying his very best to help the Power Squad work as a team, instructing each member on how they can help one another. That is, until Roborg interrupts...

> Once the context of the scene is understood, you can use this page to inspire and inform work in any of the areas we have covered in this chapter:

Fact finding

o   Who does the Cosmic Soldier apologise to?

o   Which eye has Roborg had replaced with a laser?

o   How many heroes are in the Power Squad?

Inference-based comprehension

o   What does the phrase "Enough talk" mean?

o   Why does Cosmic Soldier apologise?

o   What does Starcomet's facial expression say about his mood in the last pictures?

Word/sentence level work

o   Write a personification sentence to describe the weather in this scene.

o   Write out and correctly punctuate the dialogue for this scene.

o   Create a show-not-tell simile to describe Starcomet's emotions in the final picture.

Short writing tasks

o   Convert this scene into a detailed written narrative.

o   Turn this scene into a drama script, including stage directions.

o   Write the continuation of this scene, including a mix of direct and indirect speech between the remaining team members.

Long writing tasks

o   Rewrite the scene, extending backwards and forwards, from the first person perspective of one of the characters.

o   Use the scene to write a news script for a special report on the emergent Superhero group known as the "Power Squad".

o   Rewrite the scene and change the mood; have all the characters co-operate and work together.

Although this list of questions is not exhaustive, you can already see the variety of exercises that can be generated using a single page from a comic as the initial stimulus. This demonstrates the versatility and usefulness of comics, and even more reassuring is the fact that while these activities come from a single comic page, more than 30,000 comics have been published by the DC Comics company alone. As such, you can guarantee that you will never run out of comic stimuli to use to improve a whole range of reading, comprehension and writing skills!

CHAPTER 3
DEVELOPING PLOT AND STORY STRUCTURE THROUGH COMICS

PLANNING EFFECTIVE NARRATIVES

A well conceived, clear and comprehensive plan is the foundation of an effective narrative. Primarily, it helps writers to establish and maintain narrative cohesion – a 'must have' if they hope to keep the reader's attention. It also helps writers to decide the appropriate level of detail for their work (both the detail lifted from the sources from which the writers are drawing, and the detail the writers then decide is appropriate for their target audience.) Lastly, an efficiently organised plan enables writers to begin and end their tale effectively, with captivating openers and resolutions that transcend the 'happily ever after'. Planning also helps writers to gauge an appropriate narrative length, sequence and time frame. In this chapter we will develop planning skills and techniques that allow pupils to identify and extract elements of a sequence of action / stimulus and use them to plan an effective narrative as previously described, in keeping with a predetermined, curriculum-based, authorial agenda.

ACTIVITY 3.1: A STELLAR WARRIOR STORYBOARD
USING COMICS TO PLAN STORIES

Typically, we are taught from a young age that a story needs a beginning, middle and an end. In our own teaching we might advance this idea using something akin to the four-point structure: introduction, problem, climax and resolution. The latter model is particularly useful when developing more complex narratives. There is a risk, however, that they leave too much narrative space for the writer to 'flesh out'; they can be ineffective planning tools. These empty spaces can easily turn into incoherent chasms full of 'filler' and wasted opportunities. We can solve this by extending the planning points using a comic storyboard. This helps to focus the narrative, using key events and actions which will best convey the story, whilst helping the child to avoid simply filling space or losing track. It also allows pupils to better plan texts with preconceived agendas and conventions. To introduce this technique we will look at the story of Jack Stevens, who would become America's greatest hero during WW2, tying in nicely with fiction units such as 'stories with a historical setting' as well as faction (linking fact and fiction in a historical context).

> Share the character biography for Jack Stevens (opposite) with your class.

> Explore and discuss the military report to ensure your group has a clear understanding of the character and events. You might use the following questions to guide the discussion:

- Who was Jack Stevens?
- Was Jack special? Why?
- When did these events take place, and what was happening at the time?
- Was it surprising that Jack was chosen for the Stellar Warrior Programme? Why?

Classification: Above Top Secret

Document code: 0641 — 7YHU- 7HSS

Subject: Stevens, Jack

Height: 5' 2

Weight: 95 lbs

D.O.B.: 04.07.1917

Known Medical Ailments: 4F Classification - Asthma, Muscular and skeletal frailty, Hayfever, Heart palpitations, Crohn's disease.

Relatives: John and Denise Stevens (Deceased)

Biography:

Born to Irish immigrant parents, Jack Stevens was raised in the Lower East Side of Manhattan, New York. Both his father and mother died before he turned 18. After completing high school he enrolled as a politics student.

In the summer of 1940, owing to his strong patriotic stance, Stevens attempted to enlist in the U.S. Army to fight Nazi forces in Europe. He was classified 4F — the lowest grouping, and rejected on account of his numerous medical conditions. Stevens then attempted enlistment in eight other cities, often using false details, and was rejected each time. Stevens would later express the frustration he felt, watching friends and acquaintances leave to fight, some reluctantly, whilst he was repeatedly denied his most passionate ambition.

This tenacity in the face of such adversity gained him the attention of the genetic scientist, Professor Frederick Eberstark, head of a project to create the perfect warrior. Eberstark offered Stevens a chance to volunteer for his experimental programme. He immediately accepted.

After a rigorous and punishing selection process, Stevens was chosen to be the first experimental subject. He was given the Stellar Warrior Formula and exposed to bursts of 'Beta-Rays' which stabilised the effects of the drug, namely superhuman strength, speed, agility, healing and endurance. Upon the completion of the process, Eberstark was assassinated by a Nazi spy, leaving Jack Stevens as the first and only Stellar Warrior.

> Once the pupils have a firm understanding of the 'facts' of the story, and have made inferences that demonstrate an understanding of the motivations and experiences of the protagonist, the concept of the 'eight-frame comic planner' can be introduced using the incomplete example opposite.

> Explain that the eight-frame comic planner works by using the **image** to represent the key idea that the writer wants to embed in the readers' minds during that phase of the text. The **caption box** underneath works to sum up that part of the story, so that the writer has a well defined idea of the direction and content of that part of the narrative. The **additional features**, such as speech bubbles or onomatopoeic words (e.g. the 'whump' of the stamp) are reminders of exciting aspects that the writer may want to include in that phase. These can include things like exciting verbs or adjectives, ideas for dialogue, characteristics and information about the setting.

> Instruct the children that they will use the Jack Stevens Military Fact File, combined with the existing example cells (comic 'boxes') and their own imaginative inferences to complete the eight-frame comic planner for the historical story of Jack Stevens. Without initially realising it (as they will hopefully be far too engrossed in the excitement of creating their own comic), the pupils will already be developing planning and sequencing skills. Already, they are methodically and analytically selecting elements from a source text that suits the agenda you have given them. Further, they are ordering, editing and embellishing those elements in order to construct an engaging, clear and imaginative narrative plan. **Just ensure that they know it is not an art competition – stickmen will do!**

> Once completed, ask the pupils to share their plans with each other and then use them to create dramatic friezes for each cell. This will show the pupils whether or not their plans contain enough information to give them a clear idea of narrative content and direction for their writing, whilst developing dramatic empathy. This will also help them to create interesting, engaging characters by assuming the frame of reference of the protagonist.

> When you are happy that the group has a clear idea of the narrative, as demonstrated by the content of their plans, ask them to use their eight-frame comic planner to create a 'plot skeleton.' Set a **two-sentence** limit for each planning point to avoid the pupils writing a full narrative at this stage. Use the example on page 54 to show how their new plans relate to, yet develop, the four-point structure. Then, share the story starter to show what can be done when their (now more effective) plans are followed precisely.

1. We can't win this war!	**2.** TRO SMAE Please give me a chance.
1941, WW2, the world is in chaos, and the U.S. military panic as they discover Nazi plans for the ultimate weapon.	In New York, Jack Stevens, a sickly, frail young patriot is rejected from the U.S. army for the ninth time.
3. US ARMY RATING APPROVED WHUMP	**4.**
Dr. Frederick Eberstark, leader of a top secret military programme, recognises Jack's special qualities and offers him a chance.	Jack undergoes strenuous training, it is almost too hard but...
5.	**6.**
Jack is taken into the lab and...	Jack Stevens is transformed into...
7.	**8.**
Dr. Eberstark...	Jack realises...

PLOT SKELETON
(The 'bare bones' of the story)

For a whole book on plot skeletons and their use, take a look at *Writing Exciting Ghost Stories: Age 9 Plus – Ghost Story Plot Skeletons* by Alan Peat and Julie Barnfather.

Introduction

> WW2 has thrown the world into chaos: the Nazi regime is developing the ultimate weapon and the U.S. Army must do something.

> Jack Stevens, a sickly but brave young man, is desperate to fight for his country, but is constantly rejected.

Problem

> Dr. Frederick Eberstark, the leader of a top secret U.S. military program, recognises Jack's good qualities and gives him a chance in the army.

> After rigorous training that is almost too much to take, Jack is selected for the Stellar Warrior initiative.

Climax

> Jack is taken into the lab to undergo the process of becoming a Stellar Warrior: he does not know what this involves.

> Jack is transformed into the ultimate soldier, twice as strong, fit, fast and resilient as any other human.

Resolution

> Dr. Eberstark is assassinated by a Nazi spy sent to sabotage the Stellar Warrior programme.

> Jack realises his responsibility and becomes The Stellar Warrior.

NARRATIVE EXAMPLE BASED ON THE NEW PLANNING FORMAT

The year is 1941, and the entire civilised world has been thrown into blood-spattered, violent chaos. Armed forces claw at each other's throats, baying for blood. The Nazi military threaten to infiltrate, overtake and infect the global population with a message of hate and discrimination. To make matters worse, the United States government has discovered that the secret Deep Science division of the Nazi regime is developing an ultimate weapon. Details are sketchy, but they have discovered the code name...world-ender. America needs a world-saver, and quick.

Whump! The stamp fell down yet again, landing with the same sickening thud. It left an imprint that simply read 'Rejected'. If he hadn't been so determined, Jack Stevens probably would have been used to that word by now. No one would blame him after nine army application rejections in nine different cities. But Jack was different. Whilst those around him did all they could to dodge the draft, or embarked reluctantly to serve their time, Jack longed to be a soldier. The chance to serve, to protect, to save and defend: that is what Jack Stevens prayed for.

by Laurenne, Age 10

ACTIVITY 3.2: PLANNING FOR EVERY EVENTUALITY
TELLING STORIES FROM DIFFERENT PERSPECTIVES

In order to extend the pupils' skills in selecting, editing and ordering information in line with a brief, you may ask them to use the exact same stimulus to complete a blank eight-frame comic planner (Appendix 3) for a different character perspective or agenda. For example, you could ask them to:

> Tell the story from the first person perspective (as Jack Stevens or Dr. Eberstark).

> *Tell the story with Dr. Eberstark as the focal character. (Example 1 below)*

> Tell the story from the perspective of one of the other rejected Stellar Warrior recruits.

> *Tell the story from the perspective of the Nazi spy. (Example 2 below)*

> Tell the story from the perspective of the Army general who trains Jack Stevens.

You could extend this further by asking them to plan for different text types:

> Tell the story in diary form (Jack's or Dr. Eberstark's).

> Write the story as a news report.

> Write the story as a script for a drama performance.

> Change the setting of the story to an imaginary world.

> Include a flashback in the story (we will return to this later in the chapter).

> Change the setting of the story to a local area.

) – Dr. Eberstark as the focal character.

:roduction

As the threat from Nazi forces increases, the U.S. Army enlist German asylum seeker Dr. Frederick Eberstark to help with the development of a new breed of soldier.

Dr. Eberstark shares his background with some of his colleagues and tells how Nazi scientists tried to force him to help them modify their soldiers.

oblem

Dr. Eberstark trawls the recruitment centres all over the East Coast of America but cannot find a suitable subject for his tests; they all seem too arrogant, stupid or just plain crazy.

Having almost given up hope, Eberstark spots a young sickly man, who although frail, shows the attitude Eberstark knows will make him the perfect recruit. The doctor helps him into the Army.

max

Eberstark fights for Stevens, who struggles bravely through the training, to be selected for the Stellar Warrior programme, and eventually he succeeds.

Dr. Eberstark and his team perform the process on Stevens, successfully turning him into the ultimate soldier.

:solution

Dr. Eberstark is assassinated by one of his own assistants, a fellow German asylum seeker who was actually an undercover Nazi spy.

Jack Stevens, now known as The Stellar Warrior, vows to avenge Dr. Eberstark and prove that his research and efforts were not in vain.

(2) – From the perspective of the Nazi spy.

Introduction

> In its quest for world domination and absolute power, Nazi forces discover a plot by the Americans to prevent their development of the ultimate weapon.

> In response, the German army plan a secret infiltration mission using Max Hitzig, a German scientist, living in New York.

Problem

> The Nazi leaders recruit Hitzig, convincing him that Dr. Eberstark, a fellow German scientist, was the traitor who was responsible for the military attack on his home village some years before; the one that forced him to flee overseas.

> Hitzig uses his asylum-seeker status and work experience to gain the trust of Eberstark, who eventually hires him as a research assistant.

Climax

> Whilst searching for secret information, Hitzig discovers the Super Soldier programme. He reports his findings to the Nazi leaders, who give the order to kill Eberstark.

> Hitzig picks his moment and assassinates Eberstark just after the Stellar Warrior programme is completed, then he flees with stolen research data.

Resolution

> Hitzig manages to transmit the data but is pursued and stopped by The Stellar Warrior. Hitzig takes a cyanide pill before he can be interrogated

> Unbeknown to the U.S. army, Hitzig managed to send crucial information before his death. The Nazis know that The Stellar Warrior exists and are already plotting his demise.

By revisiting (and, in turn, revising and reinforcing) previously taught text types, pupils will discover that it is possible to manipulate the same source material to plan narratives that suit a wide variety of purposes, agendas and text types. This is a key skill that we will look to develop throughout this chapter.

ACTIVITY 3.3: HOW BORING CAN YOU GET?
PLANNING FOR EXCITEMENT

As an extra exercise in the manipulation of source material, ask your class to plan two stories using the Jack Stevens source text; one to put you to sleep, and the other to wake you up!

> Ask the group to complete the eight-frame comic planner (or go straight to extended planning points if you prefer) selecting eight frames that make the character's exploits look as mundane and tedious as possible.

> Once this is complete, challenge them to do the opposite, where every single detail is as action-packed as possible; even those which might be considered 'everyday' occurrences.

Use the following starters to model planning expectations:

Boring Story

Introduction

> Jack Stevens is obsessed with getting into the army; it's all he talks about. He leaves his few remaining friends to try yet again to enlist in the forces.

> Jack is once again rejected; the doctors give him the same old explanation. He is too small, too sick, and too weak, but Jack just won't take the hint.

Problem

> A scientist named Eberstark spots Jack after his latest rejection and says he might have an opportunity for Jack to get into the army. He then questions Jack at length about his parents, his childhood, where he grew up, his favourite foods, and a whole host of other subjects. Jack almost nods off halfway through his questioning.

> etc

Super-Duper-Exciting Story!

Introduction

> The U.S army base in Washington is attacked and infiltrated by Nazi assassins. One is captured and confesses to a plot to develop the ultimate weapon, one capable of destroying the world!

> Meanwhile in New York, young patriot Jack Stevens is rejected by yet another army recruitment centre, but not before he has been beaten up by someone twice his size, who he overheard making rude comments about American soldiers.

Problem

> Dr. Eberstark, who witnessed the attack and saw how brave and honourable Jack was, offers him the chance to join a top-secret military program, which he says will make Jack into the ultimate soldier. Jack jumps at the chance.

> etc

ACTIVITY 3.4: BUILDING A PLOT SKELETON
STREAMLINING THE PLANNING PROCESS

To allow your pupils to gain experience of using the planning skills they have developed through comics in a wider, more 'realistic' sense, provide them with the following source text on Audie Murphy, a man who is widely regarded as the most-decorated American soldier of World War Two:

THE STORY OF AUDIE MURPHY

Audie Murphy was born to a poor Irish sharecropper and his wife in 1924. He grew up as one of twelve children. He lived on farms in Texas. In 1936, Audie's father abandoned him and his family. Audie dropped out of school to help support his loved ones by working on any farm that would hire him. During this time he became a skilled marksman, shooting small game to help feed his family. Although he worked as hard as he could, he was forced to put some of his siblings in foster-homes.

Following the attack on Pearl Harbour in 1941, Audie became intent on joining the military so he could defend his country. On his first attempt he was rejected for being under age. He obtained a fake birth certificate, but was then rejected by the Marines and Paratroopers on subsequent attempts for being too short and underweight. The Navy also rejected him because of his weight. Eventually the Army accepted him and he was sent to begin his training. During an early drill exercise, Audie passed out. His commander attempted to have him sent to a cooks' school, but he insisted he wanted to be a soldier. His wish was eventually granted, as he completed his basic training and went on to infantry training.

Even then, Audie had to fight to see some action. His determination paid off, and, in 1943 he shipped out to Africa, where he completed more rigorous training. When he was eventually involved in the invasion of Sicily, he was quickly promoted to Corporal after killing two Italian officers who were trying to escape. After helping to secure Sicily, Audie was again promoted, this time to Sergeant, when he led a patrol that stopped an ambush by German soldiers. While fighting in Italy, Audie's skills as a soldier and combatant would earn him further promotions and awards for courage and bravery. On one occasion, Audie single-handedly took out a whole German machine-gun crew who had just killed his best friend, and then used their weapons to destroy nearby targets. This act earned him the Distinguished Service Cross. Eventually he became Company Commander following numerous additional acts of bravery and selflessness.

In January 1945, Audie's unit was involved in the Battle of Holtzwihr, and his crew was cut down from 128 men to 19. He ordered the remaining men to the rear, then climbed inside an abandoned tank destroyer which he used to cut down the German infantry, simultaneously attempting to use a landline telephone to call in reinforcements. He managed all of this with an injured leg. He continued this solo effort for an hour and then organized a counter-attack that drove the Germans back. For this heroic effort he received the prestigious Medal of Honour.

When he was asked why he decided to put his life on the line this way, he simply remarked, 'They were killing my friends.'

ACTIVITY 3.4: CONTINUED

> Ask your pupils to repeat the planning phases used for the various texts based on the story of Jack Stevens to craft plot skeletons that suit an agenda or text type of your choice. They will now be using skills and techniques, developed through comics, to plan a story based on a real-life soldier; one that provides them with a clear, organized sense of narrative direction and content, with little room for digression or wasted words. You may extend this further by providing biographical information on other interesting figures, perhaps ones who tie in to your current topic work.

SEQUENCING EFFECTIVE ACTION THROUGH EXPLORATION OF SEQUENTIAL ART

What if we were to view everyday life as a non-stop chain of events, and we asked a comic writer to convey every single action that comprised a single day? You might just end up with the longest, most mind-numbingly boring comic ever written. In reality, comic writers convey sequential action by carefully selecting and isolating only the most communicative and evocative moments. So carefully chosen and arranged are these images that the reader is able instinctively to fill the gaps between them with imagined actions, linking images and words together to tell a complete story. The skill for the comic creator is in selecting and manipulating the moments that succinctly, yet still imaginatively, convey the most crucial and informative aspects of the sequential action. This skill can also be tremendously useful to a narrative writer.

So far, in this chapter, we have developed planning skills that allow pupils to produce clearer, more detailed, and precise plans, crafted to suit a range of genres and agendas. In this section we will build upon those skills so that the pupils need not rely on the source material for their entire narrative plan. Instead, they will take inspiration from an opening stimulus and use their own inferences and imagination to create an original narrative plan. These new plans, like an effective comic, will contain the clearest, most succinct version of ideas to help construct a captivating and focused narrative.

ACTIVITY 3.5: HEAR NO EVIL, SPEAK NO EVIL...SEE PLENTY
INFERRING ACTION FROM WORDLESS COMICS

Comic writers are often brave enough to let their pictures do all the talking. Communicating a narrative clearly without any text, spoken or otherwise, is the ultimate example of the effective selection and expression of sequential actions. As such, these wordless comics can provide an excellent stimulus for writing, as they provide an idea of narrative direction whilst allowing the reader (and in this case the emergent writer) to contribute more of their own imaginative ideas than they would usually have space or opportunity to do.

> Remind the pupils of the 'eight-frame comic planner' that they used in the previous activities, discussing how it aids the construction of effective plot skeletons. Then talk about the idea of further developing their planning skills by looking at a stimulus for the 'introduction' planning points only, then they will be able to extend the remainder of the narrative in their own unique way.

> Share the wordless comic page with the group.

> Discuss the comic narrative, with particular focus on how the comic creator manages to tell this part of the story without words. Think about which images, from the thousands of minute actions, they have selected to include, and discuss how those images work to convey a sequence of events as well as an emotional tone. Develop this discussion further by considering which actions the creator has chosen to leave out and why, (for instance, why does it not show his entire dressing process, button by button?) Finally, ask the pupils to think about the final two cells, why would Strikeback possibly want to leave his disguise at home?

> Ask the children to select two cells from the Strikeback page to use as the introduction cells in their own wordless eight-frame comic planner. They do not need to be two cells that are next to each other on the page, but they must go in sequence, for example:

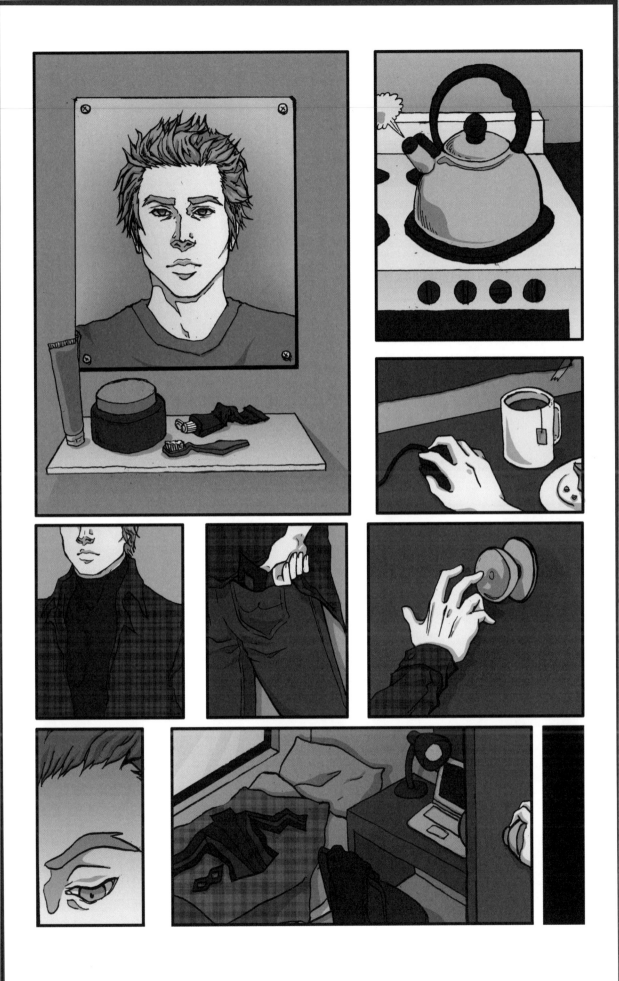

> Instruct your pupils to continue this wordless planner for all eight frames. This exercise will make them think extremely carefully about the actions they choose to use to convey their own narrative ideas as clearly and succinctly as possible. Use the following prompt questions to help if necessary:

> > Where was James Baker getting ready to go? (Look carefully at his clothes.)

> > Why does James look unsure of his own disguise?

> > What are James' emotions?

> > Why would James not want to be Strikeback for the day?

> Once completed, repeat the technique used in the previous session whereby groups and individuals swap plans and use them to create dramatic friezes that tell a wordless story. Again, this will be a good indicator of whether the pupils have chosen actions that clearly convey the events of the narrative, only this time those events will be of the pupils' own imagining.

> When you are happy that the plans are clear enough to provide a definite idea of narrative direction and content, ask the pupils to use their eight-frame comic planner to create a new plot skeleton. At this point, they will be allowed to use words! Hopefully, after the challenge of creating a wordless narrative, your pupils will relish the chance to embellish their subsequent story work with all the interesting language they had been held back from using earlier!

ACTIVITY 3.6: GET REAL!
PLANNING USING REAL-WORLD STIMULI

Once your pupils have improved their planning techniques through comics you can move on to applying those techniques to more realistic stimuli. An effective way of doing this is substituting the wordless comic stimulus for photographs.

> Share two of the sequential starter photographs (opposite) with your class:

> Discuss the images as you did during the previous activity, exploring and identifying literal actions as well as possible motivations, emotions and what the pupils think might happen next.

> Repeat the final steps from the previous activity, whereby the pupils use the two images as their 'introduction' planning points, and from these develop a wordless eight-frame comic planner, which in turn can be used to create a plot skeleton for their own story work.

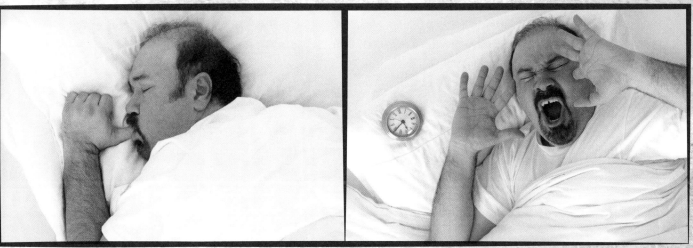

ACTIVITY 3.7: GET THE PICTURE?
CREATING YOUR OWN PLANNING STIMULUS

Extend the previous activities further by having your pupils create their own visual stimulus through drama, captured on a digital camera.

> Decide whether you want to encourage every pair/group to create their own pictures, or whether you prefer to use two or three volunteers to create a stimulus that will be used by the whole class. Ensure that whichever arrangement you decide upon, the pupils have agreed their idea with you and are supervised whilst they carry it out to ensure safe practice.

> Share the results with the class and use them in exactly the same way as before: explore, draw, plan, and then write. Your pupils will now be using effective planning techniques, developed through comics, to craft succinct story plans based on real-world stimuli, which demonstrate clear narrative direction and leave little room for meaningless deviation or filler.

Here are a few scenario ideas to get you started:

> Someone is late for an important appointment so decides to take a shortcut.

> Someone discovers a surprising object in a strange place.

> Someone is caught in a place where they should not be.

> Someone spots someone else in danger.

> Someone is preparing for a sporting competition.

> Someone gets lost whilst playing hide-and-seek.

> Someone believes they have seen a ghost.

ACTIVITY 3.8: THE FIRST PIECE OF THE PUZZLE
ENABLING INDEPENDENT STORY PLANNING

You will now look both to reduce the degree of stimulus material that you provide the pupils with and to change its position in the text. Instead of looking at two frames and using them as story starters, you will now use one frame and it will be up to you where, on the eight-frame comic planner, you ask your group to place it. For this activity you will encourage the pupils to revert to the original eight-frame comic planner format, where pictures are combined with captions, speech bubbles and other prompts.

> Share one of the following images with the class:

ACTIVITY 3.8: CONTINUED

> Discuss the picture in the same terms as you have before, but this time extend the discussion – ask the pupils what might have happened *before* the focal moment, as well as what may happen *after*.

> Instruct your group to use the image you have discussed as one of their eight-frame cartoon-planning cells. Initially it is your decision as to where they place the image. You may wish to start off by placing it in one of the '**resolution**' positions, so that your pupils will effectively have to plan in reverse. This will prepare them for thinking about stories with flashbacks in the next chapter.

> Once they have completed the eight-frame comic planner, and have written the subsequent plot skeleton, ask the pupils to pause. Instead of using the skeleton to write the story immediately, they will use the same stimulus image to create a new story by changing its position on the comic planner. If, this time, you suggest situating the image in the late '**problem**' or early '**climax**' positions, your pupils will be planning both a forward and reverse narrative. Again, this manipulation of time and order will help them with the next phase of writing. It will also demonstrate, as in the first section, how the same stimulus can be utilized and adapted in many different ways to create a narrative that adheres to a variety of authorial agendas and text-type conventions.

Here are two examples of how the same stimulus (**the frozen alien**) can produce two entirely different narrative plans depending on its position in the text. You could use them to demonstrate the point to your class.

Introduction

> A world-class five-man mountaineering team is attempting to beat the record for the quickest ascent up Mount Everest.

> The first 3 days go well, the team makes excellent progress and the conditions are good, although one teammate suggests that something is wrong.

Problem

> On the third evening they set up camp as usual, but the worried team member tells the others that something is following them. The others tell him that it is a ridiculous idea and he just needs rest.

> The next morning they awake to find the worried team member missing. They discover his body some distance away. His eyes have been removed.

Climax

> Petrified, the team decide to stay in their camp and set a trap for what they assume is a wild animal. They wait for hours until suddenly something springs the trap.

> They try to drag the creature into an empty tent, but it is too quick and escapes into the darkness. That night, all but one of the crew members disappear.

Resolution

> The next morning the remaining crew member finds the remains of his team, all with their eyes removed. He discovers a cave in a rock face and inside he uncovers what he believes to be a dead alien buried in the ice.

> As he inspects the creature more closely, it springs into life, jumping at him, aiming straight for his eyes...

Introduction

> In the surrounding hills of a snowy town a group of boys are having a snowball fight. They venture further away from the houses, up the hill and into the snowy forest.

> One of the boys dares another to climb the hill all the way up to the abandoned logging station, which is believed to be haunted.

Problem

> The boy accepts, not wanting to be thought a coward, and makes his way up, with the others following at a distance. As he reaches the watchman's hut he falls through into a tunnel that has been covered with snow.

> He hurts his leg badly, but is distracted from the pain when he discovers what he thinks is an alien body buried in the ice.

Climax

> The other boys finally get to the tunnel, and, upon discovering their friend's predicament, argue over whether to go back and get help (causing them to get into trouble) or stay and try and help him out themselves.

> They decide to go for help, and whilst they are away the boy in the tunnel notices that the alien body has begun to glow a strange shade of green.

Resolution

> The boys return with the police and firemen, and a winch is set up to pull the boy out of the tunnel. He attaches himself safely and drags the alien body up with him, but as the harness reaches the mouth of the tunnel, both boy and alien have disappeared.

> That night there are reports from neighbouring villages that a strange, green, glowing object has been spotted floating across the night sky.

MODIFYING NARRATIVE STRUCTURE FOR EFFECT

Our aim, so far in this chapter, has been the development of planning skills that help pupils to avoid meaningless digression and provide a clear and fixed sense of narrative direction. We have done this by providing the means to bridge the gaps between planning points, by facilitating increased detail in planning, and by implementing a clear, systematic, visual planning approach to ensure that the narrative stays 'on track'.

Now, however, we will actually start to encourage digression and disorder, but only that which is purposeful and engaging. Once pupils are confident with sequential planning, we will want to help them to transcend the linear narrative structure and instead start to modify the sequential nature of events to create more engaging, thought-provoking narratives.

ACTIVITY 3.9: ACTIVATE THE PLOT DE-SCRAMBLER
USING COMICS TO MANIPULATE NARRATIVE PLANS

Introduce the idea that changing narrative order can help engage readers by making them ask questions, which in turn leads to a desire to read on and 'figure things out'. However, in the version you have found, the writer has got a little carried away with plot reordering, and the pupils must help to remedy this.

> Share the scrambled plot skeleton below with your class:

A Nazi spy, sent to sabotage the Stellar Warrior programme, assassinates Dr. Eberstark.

Dr. Frederick Eberstark, the leader of a covert U.S. military experiment, recognises Jack's qualities and helps him enlist in the army.

During training, Jack suffers a twisted ankle, a broken nose, a sprained wrist and three concussions.

Jack Stevens, a weak and sickly patriot, is desperate to fight for his country. He is rejected eight times.

Jack's new uniform is red, white and blue; it represents his home and his patriotic passion.

As the only Stellar Warrior in existence, Jack realises what he must do and becomes The Stellar Warrior.

Dr. Eberstark is nervous about the process, but tries as best he can to hide this from Jack.

Jack is altered into the ultimate soldier, twice as fit, strong, fast and tough as any other human.

Jack makes his journey to the lab to undergo the experiment and become a Stellar Warrior. He still does not know exactly what will happen.

Jack travels to Dr. Eberstark's lab in an armoured car driven by a soldier named 'Johnny.'

WW2 has thrown the world into violent panic. The Nazi scientists are developing an ultimate weapon. The U.S. Army must take action.

After rigorous, painstaking training, Jack Stevens is chosen to become the first Stellar Warrior.

> Allow your class to recognize the fact that this story, although familiar in its details, does not make sense. Tell them that you believe it does make sense and they need to prove you wrong – what detailed statements and examples can they give that prove that this text isn't in order? (E.g. "It is not in order because Eberstark can't help Jack enlist in the army **after he has been assassinated**.") By doing this, the pupils are beginning to consider *cause and effect*, a concept that will play an important part in the later activities of this chapter.

> Extend this discussion by deciding, with reasons, which statements are absolutely necessary to convey the narrative and which are superfluous. Both of these verbal activities will demonstrate that when the structure of a narrative is modified, clarity must always be carefully considered.

> Using the jumbled plan, encourage the pupils to write an accurate, correctly ordered plot skeleton, removing any points they believe to be surplus to requirements. They should end up with an eight-point plan that can be used for the next set of activities.

ACTIVITY 3.10: DROP THEM IN IT
CREATING EXCITING STORY OPENERS

An effective, yet relatively simple way to begin modifying narrative structure is by using a flashback to create an exciting opener. This technique works by selecting a moment of intense action from the sequential plot skeleton and moving that moment to the start of the text to form the opener. Thus, instead of introducing all the narrative elements in the 'normal' sequential manner, the writer surprises and instantly engages the reader by dropping them right into the middle of the action, with no idea who they are reading about or where they are. After revealing just enough detail to allow reader to orientate themselves, the writer stops short of revealing all the explanatory details, having instilled the desire to 'read on' in their now-captivated audience.

> Share the story openers (opposite) with your class:

> Discuss what makes these openings effective, with particular focus on what they make the reader want to know. Extend this discussion by introducing the concept of the 'hook'. These exciting narrative openers all contain a hook, that is, a certain amount of information allowed to the reader that interests and intrigues them, leaving them with questions they want to be answered. Ask the pupils to identify the 'hooks' in these examples and explain to you what the reader is left wanting to know.

> Using the reordered plan from the previous activity, ask the pupils to pick an action from one of the planning points and use it to write an exciting flashback starter that includes a hook and leaves their reader with questions to answer. If necessary, provide them with the modelled examples. You could also work as a class to identify a bank of key actions from the plan from which they could choose.

The tall, metal cylinder hissed and groaned; its doors began to open. It was a heavy piece of machinery, one clearly designed to hold something incredibly powerful. A bluish gas escaped from inside, falling dense upon the grated floor and swirling outwards like a smoky serpent as the pod revealed its contents. The scientist gazed upon the figure inside with a look as if they'd seen a ghost. Or a god. They weren't sure which just yet...

3 months earlier...

"Stop! You're only making this worse!" Jack Stevens couldn't believe what he was saying. More surprisingly, he couldn't believe what he was doing; running down a speeding getaway car on foot, when only minutes before he would have passed out at the effort of sprinting a hundred metres. Dr. Eberstark's experiment had worked. Energy and power surged through every fibre in his body, and now he was determined not to let the good Doctor's killer get away...

3 months earlier...

Jack Stevens lay curled up on the dusty ground, the live grenade pressed into his skinny ribs. Of all the burly, fit and arrogant soldiers in the platoon, only skinny little Jack had been brave enough to sacrifice himself and smother the threat. As the sound of the cowardly, retreating footsteps of the other soldiers faded, Jack closed his eyes tightly, pictured his proud father and mother, and waited for the inevitable blast...

3 months earlier...

PUPIL EXAMPLES

The new and improved Jack Stevens stood and watched in horror as the person who had helped him to fulfill his lifelong dreams lay dead and lifeless on the floor. He wasn't going to let the killer escape. So he started to run...
Three months earlier...

By Jessica, aged 10

For Jack it was incredible. He finally felt complete. Every minute he looked around, doubting that he could really be surrounded by American soldiers. Within a few seconds, his mind leapt out of that daydream only to hear the sound of a live grenade dropping by his foot...

By Niamh, aged 11

Jack's eyes narrowed in anticipation. Thwack! The stamp imprinted on to the paper, revealing the only word Jack was reluctant to see... REJECTED. Disappointment settled on him like a dark fog. How many times would frail Jack Stevens be denied the opportunity he longed to receive...

3 months earlier...

The last thing Dr. Eberstark saw as he slipped away into heaven was his ultimate creation, the amazing Stellar Warrior...

4 months earlier...

By Laurenne, aged 10

ACTIVITY 3.11: A TRIP DOWN MEMORY LANE
WRITING EXPLANATORY FLASHBACKS

Once you have introduced the concept of the flashback, you can extend its use by showing your pupils how to include one in various places during the plot skeleton planning phase. These in-text flashbacks are an opportunity to give the reader additional contextual, historical and emotional information about the events of the main narrative. The real skill, however, is not in writing the flashbacks, but is in the way the writer transitions in and out of them without losing the thread of the narrative, and with it the attention of the reader.

> Begin by sharing the same eight-point, sequential plan that you used for the previous activity, but this time with three flashback additions:

WW2 has thrown the world into violent panic. The Nazi scientists are developing an ultimate weapon. The U.S. Army must take action.

Jack Stevens, a weak and sickly patriot, is desperate to fight for his country. He is rejected nine times.

Dr. Frederick Eberstark, the leader of a covert U.S. military experiment, recognises Jack's qualities and helps him enlist in the army.

After rigorous, painstaking training, Jack Stevens is chosen to become the first Stellar Warrior.

Jack makes his journey to the lab to undergo the experiment and become a Stellar Warrior. He still doesn't know exactly what will happen.

Jack is altered into the ultimate soldier, twice as fit, strong, fast and tough as any other human.

A Nazi spy, sent to sabotage the Stellar Warrior programme, assassinates Dr. Eberstark.

Jack realises what he must do and becomes The Stellar Warrior.

FLASHBACK 1

Jack remembers school football lessons, and how every time he was picked last. Yet in every game, he managed to score against boys twice his size. He didn't give up then, and he wouldn't now.

FLASHBACK 2

During the journey Jack spots a familiar alleyway, and a sharp pang creases his side. It was a spot where he was beaten up for defending a pretty, young lady. He worries about his weaknesses and wonders whether or not he is really the man for the job.

FLASHBACK 3

The assassin's real name is Max Hitzig, and the anger he feels towards Eberstark is due entirely to the lies he was told by the Nazi leadership. Hitzig was convinced that secrets leaked by the doctor had led to the destruction of his hometown and the death of his wife, and now he would have revenge.

ACTIVITY 3.11: CONTINUED

> Using the example, demonstrate that the first step in creating an effective flashback is to pick an event, an emotion, or an action and then think about what circumstances could have led to it. These ideas need not be based on textual evidence, instead they will rely more on the pupils' inference-making skills and imagination. Once they have chosen an aspect and come up with a plausible explanatory event for it, they will write the idea as a planning point (following the modelled example) and will decide where it will fit into the plan.

> As mentioned previously, one of the most important aspects in making a flashback work is the transition into and out of it. Share the following example with your group:

> ... But Jack was different. Whilst those around him did all they could to dodge the draft, or embarked reluctantly to serve their time, Jack longed to be a soldier. To serve, to protect, to save and defend, that is what Jack Stevens prayed for. Jack had never been one to shy away from a challenge. As he sat on the steps outside the recruitment office, he remembered all those times he'd be picked last in football games, rejected until someone simply had to take him. Even so, in every single game he managed to score against boys almost twice his height and at least three times his strength, no matter what punishment they put him through. Jack wasn't a quitter then, and he wasn't a quitter now. He would keep on trying. Jack stood up, dusted himself off and was about to continue on his way when he was stopped by an official-looking man wearing a laboratory coat and spectacles.

> "My name is Dr. Eberstark," he uttered, in a strong German accent...

> The orange text indicates the transitions that take the reader into and out of the flashback, while the green text is the flashback itself. Discuss with the class how the writer includes transitional phrases that compare one period of time with another, informing the reader that they are about to deviate from the linear narrative and take a trip down memory lane. Likewise, when this trip is finished, the writer includes a short comparative section which prepares the reader to return to the 'normal' narrative.

> To allow them to practise this transitional technique, ask them to start by creating their own transitional phrases to replace the ones in the example. You may model some yourself to support their work. Here are some examples to help:

Jack had experienced rejection before, it was nothing new to him, and as he sat there on the steps he remembered...

Jack was used to the feeling of not having his prayers answered though; he knew that you only got what you worked for in this world. As he sat there on the steps he remembered...

Struggling to get what he wanted, struggling to prove himself, everything had always been a struggle for Jack, and as he sat there on the steps he remembered...

So what if these army boys were the same? They may be bigger and stronger, but Jack knew he had what it took. He stood up, dusted himself off and...

Jack had heard the Army was all about punishment, and he doubted whether there was anyone better qualified to take on the challenge than him. He stood up, dusted himself off and...

But this wasn't a game, this was real life, and Jack was more determined to win than ever. He stood up, dusted himself off and...

> Once the pupils demonstrate confidence in moving in and out of flashbacks, and have a clear idea of what the flashback will contain, allow them to edit their previous stories to include these new features. By this stage they will be using advanced planning techniques to support writing that demonstrates an ability to manipulate the linearity and time frame of a narrative.

ACTIVITY 3.12: LEAVE 'EM HANGING
CREATING EFFECTIVE STORY ENDINGS

Comic books are often serialised, meaning they are released at regular intervals (weekly, biweekly, monthly etc.) in the form of relatively short editions. This necessitates the generation of a loyal fan base that will continue buying the comics and follow the storyline, even if they have to wait up to a month for the next instalment. One of the many ways comic writers do this is through the use of cliffhangers, yet another technique that pupils can adopt!

A simple but effective way to introduce the cliffhanger ending is through the authorial question. This works by establishing a relatively calm, resolved state at the end of a narrative, and then adding a rhetorical question that sows the seed of doubt in the reader's mind as to just how resolved matters actually are.

> Share the following cliffhanger question endings with your group:

Jack knew what he had to do. He must become The Stellar Warrior, the symbol of a great nation, and the protector of the people of the United States. After all, he was the only Stellar Warrior in existence.

Or was he?

Dr. Eberstark was dead, gone, lost to the world, and his Stellar Warrior secrets were lost with him.

Or were they?

Although saddened by the loss of Dr. Eberstark, Jack thanked his lucky stars that the Nazi spy had not managed to transmit the Stellar Warrior secrets before his death.

Or had he?

> Discuss with your group how the above examples work. Explain that first the writer must identify something in the text that, if it turned out not to be true, would impact greatly on the future of the narrative (have the pupils work out what this aspect was in the modelled examples).

> Revisit the pupils' previous story work (which should now include an exciting flashback opener as well as explanatory flashbacks throughout) and allow them to edit the ending to include an authorial question cliffhanger based on the examples you have analysed together.

> Extend this with the more sophisticated 'suggestive' cliffhanger, where instead of an authorial question, an alternate reality is merely hinted at by the author. Compare the examples opposite with the examples you have just looked at to see how they differ:

Jack knew what he had to do. He must become The Stellar Warrior, the symbol of a great nation, and the protector of the people of the United States. After all, he was the only Stellar Warrior in existence, he was sure of that. Sure that is, until the events of the very next morning.

Dr. Eberstark was dead, gone, lost to the world, and his Stellar Warrior secrets were lost with him. Or at least that's what he wanted the U.S. Army to believe.

Although saddened by the loss of Dr. Eberstark, Jack thanked his lucky stars that the Nazi spy had not managed to transmit the Stellar Warrior secrets before his death. Far away, in the bunker of a Nazi deep-science-research facility, a technician thanked his lucky stars that the data transmitter had just beeped into life.

> Again, discuss how these cliffhangers work, and how they are similar to/differ from the authorial question examples. Demonstrate how, initially, they work in the same way; by selecting an aspect that, if changed, would affect the future of the narrative greatly. Then show how this technique differs; instead of presenting the alternative reality as a question to the reader, it is instead hinted at as part of the narrative.

> Once you have made the process clear via explanation, discussion and modelled examples, allow your group to practise these more sophisticated endings before revisiting their previous story work and editing their resolution to include this new feature.

ACTIVITY 3.13: THROW IT IN REVERSE
MANIPULATING NARRATIVE TIMELINES

As a final exercise in manipulating narrative timelines, set your pupils the following challenge:

"Can you tell the story of Jack Stevens in reverse?".

Show them the following reversed, simplified plan and ask them if there is any way, perhaps by changing small details, to make the story make sense in the order shown?

1. Jack Stevens becomes The Stellar Warrior, the world's ultimate soldier.

2. Dr. Eberstark, who is responsible for the Stellar Warrior programme, is assassinated by a Nazi spy.

3. Jack is transformed, giving him superhuman speed, agility and strength.

4. Jack is taken to the laboratory to undergo the experiment.

5. Jack completes the training and is selected to be the first Stellar Warrior.

6. Dr. Eberstark helps Jack enlist in the Army.

7. Jack's army application is rejected for the ninth time.

8. The U.S. government looks for a way to defend against the Nazi threat during WW2.

This may perplex even the most able pupils, but through the inclusion of plot devices (small changes and techniques that will counter the apparent incoherent aspects of the narrative), it is possible to write a completely different story based on the same planning points.

> Share this modified plan, which includes subtle changes to help the story make sense:

1. Jack Stevens becomes The Stellar Warrior, the world's ultimate soldier.

2. Dr. Eberstark, who is responsible for the Stellar Warrior program, is assassinated by a Nazi spy who had contacts and accomplices within the U.S. Army.

3. In an attempt to discover these traitors, Jack is transformed again, removing his superhuman speed, agility and strength, allowing him to pass as 'normal'.

4. Jack leaves the laboratory after the experiment.

5. Jack enlists in Army training and works to find the traitor in the platoon.

6. After failing to find the traitor, an Army scientist helps Jack to leave the forces.

7. Jack applies for the Navy instead, and his applications are constantly rejected.

8. The U.S government continues to look for a way to defend against the Nazi threat during WW2.

> Identify the changes that have been made to the plan and discuss how each one works as a plot device to help the narrative make sense. Once your pupils have a clear idea of the direction of the new narrative, ask them to use the reverse plot skeleton to write a brand-new story, one which includes an exciting 'hook' opener, flashbacks throughout, and finishes with a suggested cliffhanger ending. Your class will now be combining all their improved planning skills into one text, which you can use as the basis to expand into other stories from any fictional genre.

CHAPTER 4
DEVELOPING CHARACTERISATION THROUGH COMICS

EXPANDING CHARACTER 'TYPES' VIA COMIC CHARACTER STUDY

Comics are sometimes perceived to be simple stories, solely concerned with the struggle between good guys (superheroes) and bad guys (super villains.) However, the long-standing success of many comic characters comes, in part, from their propensity to blur that moral line which at first seems so clear. Iron Man habitually rebels against authority; Spider-man struggles with his responsibilities; the X-Men are outcasts, and Batman is scorned by the people he tries to protect. As such, comics provide an opportunity to explore and expand fictional characters beyond ideas of 'good' and 'bad,' concepts that are restrictive for pupils when creating their own characters. Not only that, but the wealth of literature surrounding these characters makes them an ideal subject for character study. One is only ever a Google or a Wiki search away from uncovering a character's history, genesis, life, actions and more.

ACTIVITY 4.1: NOT JUST 'GOOD' OR 'BAD'
EXPANDING PERCEPTIONS OF CHARACTERS

Using online Marvel and DC Comics Wiki's, find and examine characters who have crossed the good/bad divide, as well as characters who are notoriously morally ambiguous (anti-heroes.) Here are some suggestions:

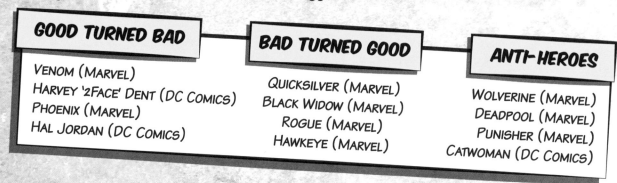

GOOD TURNED BAD

Venom (Marvel)
Harvey '2Face' Dent (DC Comics)
Phoenix (Marvel)
Hal Jordan (DC Comics)

BAD TURNED GOOD

Quicksilver (Marvel)
Black Widow (Marvel)
Rogue (Marvel)
Hawkeye (Marvel)

ANTI-HEROES

Wolverine (Marvel)
Deadpool (Marvel)
Punisher (Marvel)
Catwoman (DC Comics)

> To help delimit your pupils' envisioning of 'good' and 'bad' characters, assign a character to research to each table.

> Have half the pupils on the table prepare an argument for why the character could be seen as 'good,' and the other half an argument as to why the character could be seen as 'bad.'

> Ask them to consider the thoughts, feelings and actions of the characters, and explore their motives (relating to their back story) and their behaviour.

Through this process they will discover for themselves that characters they may have previously perceived as 'good' or 'bad' are actually much more complex, and it is this complexity that makes them interesting. This will encourage them to strive for a similarly multifaceted characterisation within their own work.

Here is an example of the start of an argument which you could use as a modelling tool, explaining why a character named Johnny 'Stitchface' Connolly, who appears to be 'bad', could be considered 'good'. This is a process which pupils could undertake for any morally vague character that interests them. This will enable them to develop persuasive writing techniques as well as empathy and motive exploration.

Although many people think Johnny 'Stitchface' Connolly is a terrible villain, we believe he has good qualities that should not be ignored. We discovered that before suffering a horrible attack at the hands of a criminal, Johnny was Megatropolis' Chief Justice, and one of the DarkSpectre's closest friends and allies. His nickname was 'Mr Shine' because of his clean-cut image, which meant he always did everything right. He was a brave man who fought for justice. Unlike DarkSpectre, he did not have the protection of a mask or armour. He was attacked by a nasty man who threw acid at him, hurting him terribly and making him angry. We think this was a fair reaction to the way he was treated, and people should not forget the many good things he did for Megatropolis.

ACTIVITY 4.2: THROUGH THE EYES OF A MENACE
DEVELOPING CHARACTER EMPATHY

George Orwell suggested that `history is written by the winners', and although we have seen that comics are unique because they explore the motives and behaviours of all characters, they are still usually written with a focus on the eponymous superhero. To help develop the ideas from Activity 4.1 regarding complex characterisation and empathy, as well as teaching pupils to use different modes of communication to reason and respond to different points, we might ask them to rewrite a comic text from the 'bad' guy's perspective.

> Pick and share a comic story where the hero prevents the completion of a villain's scheme.

> Discuss with the pupils what the villain was trying to do and why, what their motives were, and what they hoped would happen. Ask them to consider what the villain thinks of the hero.

> With these ideas shared, ask the pupils to rewrite the story in the first person, as if they were the villain, describing and explaining their actions, what they hoped to achieve, and why they believed they are doing the right thing.

> They could even reveal an ulterior/hidden motive in the hero, making them out to be the villain, linking back to the idea of the blurred moral line whilst embedding the technique of complex characterisation.

ACTIVITY 4.3: YOURS SINCERELY, THE VILLAIN
WRITING IN THE FIRST-PERSON

Extend Activity 4.2 via the creation of a letter, written in character from villain to hero, explaining the actions of the villain. In doing this the pupils will be developing their ability to deduce characters' reasons for behaviour from their actions, as well as gaining experience in both the explanation text-type and the conventions of letter writing. Focus on how the pupils adopt the character of the Villain, the vocabulary they would use to speak to the Hero, and how they might even try to talk the Hero round to their way of thinking using persuasive-writing skills. This will also introduce the idea of using characteristics to inform character interactions.

Here follows an example of the beginning of an explanation letter from MagmaMan to Captain Zanthus, the leader of the Z-Men. It comes after the Captain and his team have foiled an attempt by MagmaMan to infiltrate and threaten the United States Government, which allegedly has plans to arrest and perform medical experiments on mutants:

FROM THE DESK OF MAGMAMAN

Riker's Island Penitentiary
ARDC - C-74
11-11 Hazen Street
East Elmhurst
NY 11370

The Z School for Gifted Youth
1407 Graymalkin Lane,
Salem Center,
NY 56340

Dear Zanthus,

I am writing to clear up the little 'misunderstanding' between your friends and mine last week. As you know, our Government has once again expressed its concerns about mutants. They fear us, Zanthus. They fear what they do not understand, and they know how great our powers are. Due to my concern for the survival of our race, I decided to put a spy inside the White House. They discovered a plot to arrest, or dare I say, hunt down, our brothers. They wanted to capture them, experiment on them, torture them and probably kill them. That includes the children at your precious school, Zanthus. I decided the only way to protect our kind was to attack. Sometimes that is the only thing these humans understand...

ACTIVITY 4.4: CREATING HISTORY
WRITING CHARACTER ORIGINS

Once you have found a character that your class can really get their teeth into, look at a story that does not include a character history, but does give a good sense of what that character is like, what they stand for, their attitudes, values and beliefs, whether negative or positive. Once again, through this study, your pupils are developing their ability to **deduce characters' reasons for behaviour from their actions and their ability to explore their motives.**

Subsequently, have your pupils create a back story for the character that explains the characteristics they have identified.

> As a class, mind-map ideas for potential events that made the character into the person they are today, the more creative and detailed the better.

> For those pupils who thrive on particularly challenging briefs, ask them to create a back story where the character changes their moral stance, and instruct them to describe the event that brought about the change. For example, they might find a character like Jack Jordan, the expert fighter pilot with no fear, chosen by an intergalactic police force called the 'Cosmic Military' to protect Earth from the powers of evil. They might then suggest that:

Before Jack was a fighter pilot, he was a high-school dropout who cared about no one but himself. He had a rich family and was expected to follow in the footsteps of his father, a famous technological industrialist, but instead he decided to waste his family's money on flash cars which he would often crash due to his recklessness. Then one night while out driving, Jack almost collided with another car, swerving at the last minute to avoid it and ending up upside down in the wrecked vehicle in an adjacent field. He had seen a passenger in the other car, a young girl, her eyes wide as he hurtled towards them, and as he woke up he saw these eyes looking down on him again. "It's a good job you've got fast hands, mister," the voice said. "Maybe you should be a pilot." It was then that Jack realised how precious life was, and then that he decided he was going to spend his life trying to protect it.

ACTIVITY 4.5: THE HISTORY OF CHARACTERISTICS
RESEARCHING CHARACTERS AND WRITING BACK STORIES

In creating a character with interesting characteristics, it is important that pupils explore the reasons for characters being instilled with certain qualities. Since the mid-20th century, prominent comic characters have often mirrored societal development, and there is a wealth of information regarding their origins and conceptualisation.

> Begin by exploring the creation of Captain America. Most schools study World War 2 at some point, and here is a character born directly out of that conflict. Pupils can research both the literal, contextual history of the character, and their fictional history.

> Ask pupils to find out who created Captain America, why they made him look and act the way he did, and why they gave him humble origins before making him into a Super Soldier.

> The results of this research could be presented orally, in written form, in an electronic fact file or in a group presentation, embellished with an electronic slide show.

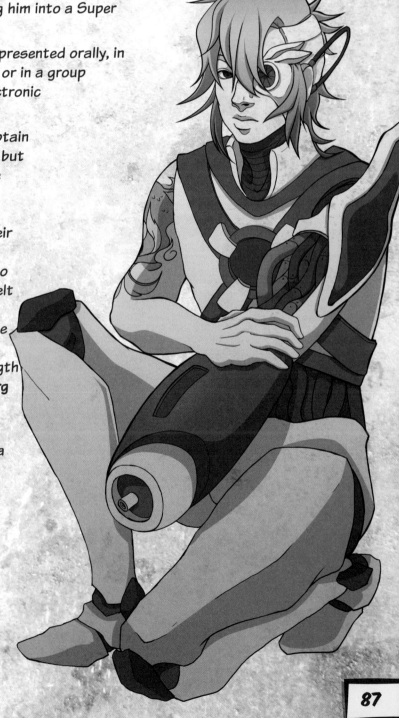

> Once this has been completed for Captain America, expand to other characters, but give the pupils a chance to infer some possible explanations behind characterisations and record these predictions before they undertake their research. Was Spider-man a nerdy weakling who became strong enough to take on anyone because his creator felt nerdy and weak in school and always wished he had the power to silence the bullies? Was Superman's strength a modern take on ancient men of strength like Hercules and Samson? Was **Roborg** a reflection of concerns over unchecked scientific advances?

> By having the pupils think about why a character was given a certain characteristic, they will learn to think more carefully and thoughtfully about the characteristics they imbue their own creations with. They are also developing the ability to infer writers' perspectives from what is written and from what is implied.

ACTIVITY 4.6: CHARACTERISTIC CONTINUATION
APPLYING CHARACTERISATION TECHNIQUES IN A WIDER CONTEXT

This activity should be the culmination of all the above activities, where pupils will read part of a comic story, examine the characters' behaviour and then use this study to inform a continuation of the story. They will look, not only to continue the events of a narrative, but to develop the narrative based on the traits of the characters.

> Take a target character, one you feel has been best received by the class, and share a partial story with them.

> Stop at a pivotal point and share ideas about what they think will happen next. Ideas must come with an explanation based on a character feature, i.e. "I think Strikeback will save the Chief because, even though he mistreats his alter ego James Baker, Strikeback does not pick and choose whom he saves. He cares about everyone."

> Use these shared ideas to create a continuation of the story, and once completed, work may be shared and compared with the ending of the original text.

> Discuss the following questions – Were the pupils' continuations accurate? Did they identify the same characterisations as the author intended the character to display? Or better still, did they create a more exciting, original continuation thanks to their imaginative use of characterisation?

CREATING MULTIFACETED CHARACTERS AND ENHANCING CHARACTER INTERACTIONS

In this chapter we have encouraged the use of comic characters as a vehicle to expand and improve the understanding of captivating characteristics. While the use of superheroes and villains is an effective means to enthuse pupils about character development, it will, unfortunately, not be appropriate to throw superheros into every story, no matter how well-rounded the characters are! This is where the **alter ego** comes in to play.

The alter ego is the comic character's 'normal' form, the way they present themselves when not in crime-fighting or crime-causing mode. Usually, it is who they are underneath their disguise. For example, underneath his iconic blue and red suit, Spider-man is really Peter Parker. Captain America is really Steve Rogers, Iron Man is Tony Stark, and so on. The exception to this rule is Superman. His alter ego provides us with a tremendously useful tool for exploring 'human' characteristics.

Superman was born as Superman. That is who he really is. His disguise, or suit, is the business suit of Clark Kent, the alter ego that Superman created in order to integrate with the human race. To fit in, Superman had to create his own set of human characteristics, and they had to be realistic and persuasive enough to convince people that he was a mild-mannered news reporter, not a super-being capable of lifting planets. This challenge that Superman faces can be a useful starting point for us to help pupils develop well rounded characters. It enables us to avoid the prevalent and restrictive 'character profile – looks, age, name and characteristics' pro forma. As we have already seen, characteristics are a complex concept, which can be made less daunting if we can provide an exciting and inspirational stimulus.

ACTIVITY 4.7: BEING CLARK KENT
USING CHARACTERISTICS TO INFORM ACTIONS

Research and discuss the characteristics of Superman's alter ego, Clark Kent. Split the class into small working groups and use both the Wiki resources and Superman comics to determine the defining characteristics of Clark Kent and to create their own superhero alter ego character (e.g. 'Jonathan Steel').

The results should be recorded as a written report, enabling pupils to think about how their character would act according to their identified characteristics. This also develops adjective, verb and adverb use and can be modelled before the task if necessary (e.g. Jonathan Steel is an extremely clumsy person. He often gets in trouble for knocking over neat piles of stationary and bumping into unsuspecting co-workers). Groups can nominate a speaker to feed back their findings to the rest of the class.

Once the characteristics have been identified, use the knowledge of the alter ego's 'human' characteristics to inform short narratives based on their reactions in certain settings and situations (see Appendix 1 for suggestions). For example:

HOW WOULD JONATHAN STEEL REACT IF...

...HE WAS ASKED TO OPEN A JAM JAR THAT NO ONE ELSE HAS BEEN ABLE TO OPEN?

Jonathan would try his best to open the jar, wrestling and struggling with it, but in the end would give up, because he isn't very strong.

ACTIVITY 4.8: ALTER-EGO ACTION
USING CHARACTERISTICS TO INFORM REACTIONS

Extend Activity 4.7 to other comic characters – start with another well-known example. Ask the pupils to find out how they try to seem 'normal'? How do they act, speak, look at and react to others? Again, once characteristics have been recorded and shared, use them to create short descriptions of interactions between an alter ego and a selection of people in a variety of places. (See Appendix 2 for people and settings.) For example:

HOW WOULD JAMES BAKER REACT IF...

...HE MET HIS TEACHER AT THE SUPERMARKET?

James would be extremely respectful and would ask if his teacher needed help with the shopping because he is a bit of a geek who enjoys school tremendously, and he wants his teachers to like him.

Expand and invert this activity with the alter ego of a villain – how would a villain fit, undetected, into society? Consider behaviour, speech, and ways in which the characters might trick people into thinking they are 'good.' etc. Shape-shifting characters like Marvel's Mystique and Loki are particularly effective here, as they adopt the exact characteristics of other people in order to deceive. For example:

HOW WOULD THE SHAPESHIFTER REACT IF...

...SHE MET A POLICE OFFICER AT THE SCENE OF A BANK ROBBERY?

The Shapeshifter would pretend to be another Police Officer, acting confidently and with authority. She would make polite, firm enquiries about what had happened so that she can sneakily find out all that the Police know.

Finally, secure the learning from these activities through drama. This will really get the pupils to think about how characteristics inform interactions as they themselves interact, in character, with each other in an imaginary setting. Begin with a character that the class knows well, both in terms of superhero and alter ego identities. Hotseat one pupil as that character, starting in hero mode, and have them react, according to their characteristics, to a variety of other people in a mixture of places. (See Appendix 2 for suggestions of both.) Decide when to switch the pupil in the hotseat into alter-ego mode, and you should see a definite change in responses based on the pupil using characteristics to inform actions.

ACTIVITY 4.9: CREATE YOUR OWN HERO
DEVELOPING MORE COMPLEX CHARACTERS

This gives your pupils the chance to use all the skills developed so far. Allow them to create their own superhero, including the normal details such as name, visual description, age etc. and then request a detailed description of the characteristics of their hero. The number of key characteristics can be differentiated appropriately, but each description should include an example of how the characteristic might influence the character to act. For example:

Renegade is a determined hero who cannot stand it if he fails at anything, even the smallest things. If he makes a mistake when fighting a criminal, he gets angry and frustrated at himself, but this often helps him to win.

Expand this by having the pupils create an alter ego for their character, following the same format, with the same expectations. Under the guise of creating secret personas they are actually creating 'normal' characters. Ones who are much more engaging and multifaceted than they may otherwise have been, and which could be used in any narrative.

DESCRIBING BODY LANGUAGE THROUGH WORDLESS COMICS

Now that the pupils are using captivating characteristics to inform actions and interactions, a further way to enhance characterisation is through the inclusion of body language. Comics are again useful for this; often conveying stories through entirely wordless sequential art, where the reader decodes the body language of the characters to understand the narrative.

You might be concerned that comics detract from reading by removing the need to imagine, and by distracting the reader from the written text with overly engrossing illustrations. Will Eisner, renowned comic writer, artist and creator of *The Spirit*, argued that the pictures actually draw the reader in further and make them want, and even need, to read the caption, as it explains the illustrations. He insisted that the two are independent. He used a fairly simple illustrated example of a figure emerging from a manhole, covered in waste and debris, in obvious distress. He then drew a blank speech bubble next to the figure, and 'defied anyone to look at that picture without wanting to know what is inside that balloon'. It is this well-made point that inspires the following activity.

ACTIVITY 4.10: FILL THE BUBBLE
ENTERING THE MIND OF YOUR CHARACTERS

This activity is useful when analysing pupils' ability to infer from body-language and it also gives pupils the opportunity to develop their ability to correctly record speech.

Look at the picture opposite and discuss it with the pupils in terms of the body-language features of the picture and what it implies, and as a result, what the character might be saying. Remind them of the way that characteristics impact on actions. The discussion may go something like this:

Teacher: Without suggesting what Strikeback might be saying in this picture, can you identify some of his body-language features? What is he doing?

Pupil: He has his head down and he is covering his face with his hand. His shoulders are hunched.

T: Great observations. Even though we don't know what Strikeback is saying, how do you think he is feeling?

P: Sad, upset.

T: How do you know? Can you give a more detailed explanation?

P: He is sad because he is hiding his face with his hand. Maybe he is ashamed of something he has done.

T: Much better, and what characteristics do we know Strikeback has that might help us figure out what he is saying?

P: We know he always tries to help people, but sometimes he doesn't like all the responsibility he has.

T: Excellent. So remembering that, what might he be saying?

P: Maybe 'I can't stand being a hero any more. It's too hard. I quit!'

Provide the pupils with different examples of comic figures in evocative poses, where body language is expressive, with blank speech bubbles. These can be easily found on the Internet and speech bubbles added in a publishing program, or taken directly from comics with speech Tipp-Exed out.

Ask pupils to fill in the speech bubbles as they did as a class, following your example. Remember to stress that they are writing what the character is saying, not what they are thinking, as thoughts are not recorded with speech marks.

Expand this activity to everyday people and situations. Do this by selecting pictures from the Internet and magazines and adding your own blank speech bubbles in the same manner as before. Once again the pupils are initially enthused by a comic-book stimulus, yet end up applying what they have learned to 'real' characters that could be used in any narrative.

ACTIVITY 4.11: TALKING BODY LANGUAGE
USING SIMILES TO CREATE MOOD

Extend Activity 4.10 by developing captivating characterisation through the inclusion of body language. One of the simplest body language principles pupils learn is that emotions are shown predominantly on the face, i.e. when we are happy we smile, when sad we cry, when angry we frown and grit our teeth. Text emoticons, :) :(>:(, further embed this idea. However, *character descriptions and interactions can be greatly enhanced by including a description of the language of the whole body.* It is also a fantastic opportunity to develop the pupils' ability to use similes.

Share an example of a wordless cell from a comic, and ask the pupils to explain the body-language features of the character, with extra praise given to those who can answer in the form of a simile. Once they have done this, ask them to infer the mood of the character. For example:

EYEBROWS POINTING DOWNWARDS LIKE TWO CROSSED SWORDS.

EYES PIERCING LIKE LASER BEAMS.

CHIN SAT HEAVY ON HIS CHEST LIKE A TEN TONNE WEIGHT.

FINGERS GRIPPING THE ARMS OF THE CHAIR AS TIGHT AS A VICE.

CAPE DISCARDED LIKE YESTERDAY'S PAPERS.

LEGS SPREAD AS LAZILY AS A SLEEPING SLOT

Starcomet's mood: Exhausted, but deep in thought and worried.

Extension: Ask the pupils to modify their mood answer in the light of the characteristics of the character, further embedding the technique of using characteristics to inform actions. For example:

> **Starcomet's mood:** Exhausted because he has to lead a double life, and deep in thought about whether lying to people about his identity is acceptable. He is worried that the people he loves may discover the truth.

Extend this further by asking them to write a speech bubble for the character, as in Activity 4.10, further embedding pupils' inference-making and speech-recording skills.

ACTIVITY 4.12: WHOLE BODY DRAMA
EXPLORING BODY LANGUAGE THROUGH ACTING

Extend Activity 4.11 using pictures of ordinary, everyday people, again linking the skills that were introduced via comic characters to more useable and 'realistic' figures. Secure the skills using drama, where pupils receive behaviour cards (see Appendix 4), assume the emotional expression using their whole body, and other pupils have to describe the body-language features and infer the emotional viewpoint. Again, give more praise if the observations are delivered in the form of a simile. In completing these exercises the pupils will have been introduced to a skill through the exciting stimuli of comic characters and yet end up applying it to create rounded characters that can be used in any narrative. They will also have improved their ability to vary pace and develop viewpoint through the use of direct and reported speech, portrayal of action and selection of detail.

CHAPTER 5
DEVELOPING LOCATIONAL WRITING THROUGH COMICS

DESCRIBING COMIC SETTINGS THROUGH AN INCREASED, MULTI-SENSORY VOCABULARY

The idea that locational writing can be the cornerstone of a narrative is a well explored one. However, this chapter will show that the most effective settings can even become characters in their own right. Comic writers are in an especially fortunate position; they have the advantage of being able to present settings visually, in all their intricacy, and combine this with text to draw the reader in further. As a result, the landscapes and architecture of comic worlds can be as memorable and affecting as their characters. Through learning about these physical creations, we will stimulate the pupil's desire for a more descriptive vocabulary, and will show how, through proficient locational writing, the 'where' can become a central character of the narrative.

ACTIVITY 5.1: BREAKING THE VOCABULARY BANK
GENERATING EXCITING LOCATIONAL VOCABULARY

Underpinning the initial step of improved locational writing is the idea that, when faced with an impressive and exciting stimulus (Starcomet's Lair, for example), most pupils will want words that do justice to their observations. If, within their current vocabulary they don't find the tools they need, rather than shying away from attempting to explain what they see and think (which they might do with a less inspirational but equally complex stimulus), they will instead enjoy the opportunity to find more appropriate words and put together phrases that fully convey their findings.

> Start by selecting an appropriate image of a comic setting.

   For the working example we will use an image of **DarkSpectre's Lair** (page opposite).

> Begin this activity by asking the pupils what they can see. This simple request will allow them to look closely at the setting, striving to explore every detail. It also allows you to establish a subjective forum, where there are no wrong answers, and where pupils will feel confident in sharing what they can see, or what they **think** they can see.

> Repeat and explain the most effective descriptive suggestions whilst giving pupils who provide limited responses the opportunity to clarify and expand their ideas. If they struggle, support them by allowing their peers to develop their ideas with them, so they see how an idea might be broadened. Conversely, if a pupil gives an overly verbose response, provide them and their peers the opportunity to offer a more concise version of the idea. As well as provoking detailed verbal explanations and cooperative appraisal, this speaking and listening exercise will provide us with many useful adjectives which you can use for the next part of the activity.

> Take one of the more simplistic adjectives, such as one which describes size and colour (big/small and dark/bright) and write it on the board. Use this as the nucleus of a mind-map and have pupils working in groups, using thesauruses, or an online visual thesaurus, to generate as many alternatives to these words as possible. How the pupils record these suggestions and how the groups are arranged is up to you, but try setting time limits and allocating rewards if your cohort thrives on competition.

> Assign other group members to look up definitions for the suggested synonyms, which will help to develop dictionary skills whilst opening up a discussion about the appropriateness of terms, ensuring that thesauruses are used effectively. These activities can also be completed using ICT word processing and dictionary software if you wish to integrate information technology into your lesson.

Let's say one of the pupils thought the Lair looked 'dark'; here is an example of how the mind-map might look:

The red words are examples of terms that might be suggested by pupils who have taken words from the thesaurus without fully considering their proper context, and will provide you with a useful means to explore and explain why not all synonyms are appropriate for every subject. To extend this, and in an attempt not to discount the suggestions of all the pupils, you may consider leading a discussion into situations in which these synonyms *could* be appropriate, e.g. *cloudy* when describing weather, and *opaque* when exploring light in a science lesson.

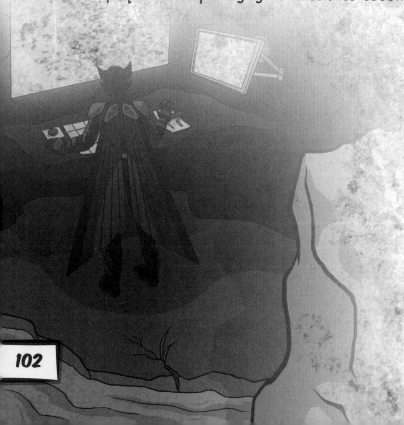

ACTIVITY 5.2: ASTONISHING ADJECTIVES
EXTENDING LOCATIONAL DESCRIPTIONS

Once you have created an adjective word bank for the setting you are exploring, explain that these words, while exciting, are not useful in isolation. They must be accurately and effectively combined in order to convey the full detail of the setting to a reader. First, establish the idea that adjectives can be combined very simply to describe the Lair.

The Lair is gloomy and foreboding.

Whilst this is better than 'the Lair is dark and not nice', it is still fairly simplistic and should be extended quickly. An easy way to do this is to reword the broader description of the setting, then add a description of a more specific detail.
For example:

The gloomy, foreboding Lair housed many powerful, hi-tech computers.
or,
The gloomy, foreboding Lair contained the iconic, menacing SpectreSuit.

As an aide-memoire for your pupils, you could give this sentence type a name, such as a 'broad then specific' sentence. Once the pupils understand how the description is constructed, you can extend this activity further by changing the opening adjectives:

The sombre, dusky Lair contained the stealthy, armoured SpectreRacer.

This descriptive exercise will allow you to generate teaching points regarding the use of close-reading to find exciting elements to describe, as well as appropriate adjective use. It will also allow you to demonstrate accurate punctuation in adjective lists and how to expand the use of interesting connectives.

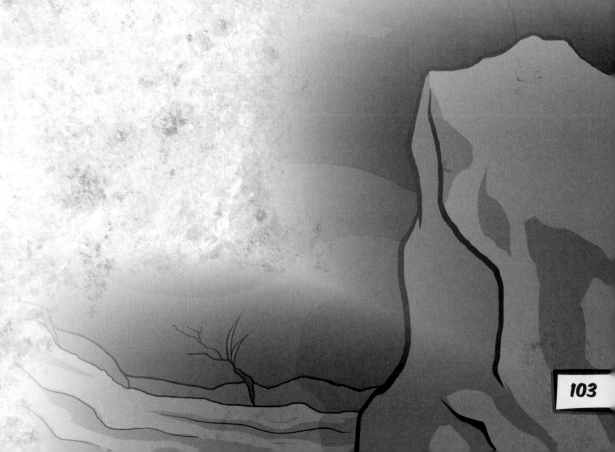

ACTIVITY 5.3: SPEAKING METAPHORICALLY
USING FIGURATIVE LANGUAGE TO DESCRIBE SETTINGS

As a stepping stone towards developing a setting that has its own character, the descriptions from the previous activity can be extended via the inclusion of similes and metaphors (describing something as having a quality in common with something quite different in every other way for dramatic effect). You may also want to draw the pupils' attention to other visual aspects, such as colour, material properties and shape, to provide them with more aspects upon which to comment. Here are some examples which show how the descriptions from the previous activity have been improved through use of simile and metaphor:

The gloomy, foreboding Lair was concealed deep underground like lost treasure. It housed many powerful, hi-tech computers, with dazzling screens that pierced the dark like lightning bolts.

or

The sombre, dusky Lair was a predator's nest. It contained the iconic, menacing SpectreSuit; the uniform of justice.

Again, this activity will not only help your pupils to expand their descriptive vocabulary and contribute to establishing settings with real character, but it will also enable them to extend their knowledge of connective use, accurate punctuation and effective phrase construction.

ACTIVITY 5.4: COME TO YOUR SENSES
CREATING MULTISENSORY DESCRIPTIONS

> Using the same mind-mapping technique as before, create banks of adjectives that could describe the setting in terms of senses other than the visual. Explain that multisensory descriptions help make the reader feel they are in the setting, alongside the character, and the more senses pupils can stimulate through their descriptions, the more immersed their reader will feel.

> A good way to generate ideas for these multisensory descriptions is through drama. Ask the pupils to go on an imaginary walk through the setting, and as they move, ask them to describe what they can hear, what they can touch, what they can smell, and even how the air might taste.

Here is an example for each sense, using similes and metaphors, which you can use to model effective multisensory descriptions:

SOUND

The tomb-like silence in the Lair was deafening, disturbed only by the soul-chilling screech of rats, the guardian soldiers of this underground fortress.

TOUCH

The daunting, jagged walls of the Lair were as coarse as sandpaper, yet the sturdy, metallic walkway was smooth and cold to the touch.

SMELL

The dingy, chilly Lair smelled of stagnant water, like a soggy jacket left out in the rain.

TASTE

The air inside the Lair tasted old and stale, an inmate in a prison of hidden troubles and concealed nightmares.

ENHANCING CHARACTER AND SETTING INTERACTION THROUGH PLACEMENT IN STIMULATING ENVIRONMENTS

The previous activities were designed to develop locational writing in terms of descriptive content. A unique, detailed and encapsulating description of setting is crucial to allow the reader to picture the imagined space. The activities in this section will help to ensure that a well-depicted setting does not merely become the 'where' in the obligatory 'who, what, when, where and why' list, relegated to background player whilst the focus switches entirely to the characters' actions and interactions with one another. Instead, we will look for the location to become a character itself, one which interacts with, affects, and is affected by, all the other characters in the narrative.

These activities will also give you the opportunity to continue the work on characteristics from the previous chapter. The setting is no longer an inert backdrop, rather it interacts, in a multisensory way, with the other characters - who themselves have their own unique characteristics.

ACTIVITY 5.5: YOU ARE THE HERO
DESCRIBING A LOCATION FROM A CHARACTER'S PERSPECTIVE

> Start by combining a comic character with whom your group is comfortable and a comic environment that you have explored during the previous activity. Extend the 'imaginary walkabout' activity by asking the pupils to do the same again, but this time in character as your chosen superhero. Ask the pupils how they feel in this setting, ask them to describe what they can sense and most importantly what they are doing and why. You may choose to model an effective description for them before they begin, for example:

The Lair is murky like a dirty puddle, and the air is thick and stale, but I move around confidently, my eyes are used to the darkness. I slump into my chair, feeling the softness cushioning my bruised and aching limbs, and it feels like a hug from an old friend. Some people would see this place as dank, foreboding and creepy, but to me these jagged walls are my home. The Lair is my protector. She keeps me safe.

ACTIVITY 5.6: LET YOUR POWERS COMBINE
COMBINING LOCATIONAL WRITING TECHNIQUES

> Once the pupils have a sense of themselves in character in these comic settings they should start to work on documenting this interaction in the third person. Introduce a new setting and ask them to use it to complete the descriptive activities from the previous section (Activities 5.1-5.4), then use the following example to show them how to combine the three elements you have been working on, which are ordered as follows:

> A multisensory description of the setting

> An explanation of how the setting makes the character feel

> What the characters subsequently do, including reasoning for these actions based on their characterisation

For this example we will be using the character of Starcomet and the setting of the Castle Chill. A colour-coded key has been included to demonstrate how the skills developed so far have been integrated:

RED WORDS — substituted words (originals in brackets) from the thesaurus exercise (Activity 5.1)

BLUE WORDS — similes and metaphors (Activity 5.3)

GREEN WORDS — multisensory descriptions (Activity 5.4)

ORANGE WORDS — character emotions (Chapter 4)

PURPLE WORDS — character actions and reasoning (Chapter 4)

KEY

Castle Chill towered above Starcomet as he strode (walked) through its cavernous (huge) opening. Its walls were made of crystals that pierced the air like a warrior's sword. These rocks, although icy and jagged in their appearance, felt strangely warm and smooth under his fingers. Peering (looking) up at the statue of his father, Starcomet could almost hear a warm voice welcoming him home, and the smell of clean air was a welcome change to the polluted (dirty) streets of Megatropolis.

Although it was merely (only) a statue, a crystal sculpture of his father, the towering (tall) figure made Starcomet feel protected. He spent so much time defending and caring for others that it was a relief for him to feel safe, cared for and loved. He finally felt like he was home.

As the relief spread over him, Starcomet began to relax his heavy shoulders, painful from the strain of all his heroic feats (actions.) He removed his cape, and although it was not heavy for such a strong being, he felt immediately free of all the worries and responsibilities that came with it. He ambled (walked) up to a large crystal and looked at his reflection, something he usually did only when checking his Jonathan Steel disguise to make sure he looked nerdy enough. But the crystal reflection showed him who he really was, a protector, and it showed him that no matter how tired he got, he must be the hero people needed him to be. Finally, the castle silently assured (told) him that this place would always be there for him, his lifelong friend, his guardian and his home.

You can use this example not only to show the pupils how to combine and structure the various aspects that they have been developing, but also to have them analyse it, either in a group or individually, to allow them to identify the features for themselves and explain how they have been used. If the pupils can describe the narrative construction to you, you can be confident that they will be able to replicate it in their writing.

ACTIVITY 5.7: REAL-WORLD HIDEOUTS
DESCRIBING REAL-WORLD SETTINGS

> Once you have completed the previous activity with a selection of settings and characters, you can begin to make the leap to more 'realistic' environments. One effective and exciting way is to use real-world places that bear a resemblance to the settings you have already looked at. For example:

Try moving Starcomet from Castle Chill into the Naica Mines, situated under Mexico's Naica Mountain in the Chihuahuan desert:

Or move DarkSpectre from the Lair to the Jeita Grotto in the Lebanon Mountains

> These subtle changes will enable the pupils to begin applying the skills they have developed through the comic stimulus to real-world settings. They will also, depending on your cohort, allow you to have fun convincing them that 'explorers have discovered the real Castle Chill'! You can extend this further by introducing locations from your local area, visits to which would greatly enhance the dramatic walkabout activity and provide pupils with tactile inspiration for their locational writing.

ACTIVITY 5.8: THE REALLY REAL WORLD
DESCRIBING EVERYDAY SETTINGS

> The next step in developing locational writing skills that can be applied to any narrative is to revisit the idea of the 'alter ego' in the real-world setting from the previous chapter. By placing well-rounded alter ego characters into vividly imagined locations and exploring how they interact, the pupils will be one step closer to comfortably locating **any** character into **any** setting and giving a detailed, reasoned and imaginative account of the interaction. Here is an alter-ego example to show how locational writing skills learned through comics might be applied to a 'normal' setting:

The hectic newsroom at 'The Megatropolis Reporter' was a real beehive of activity. Headlines rang out and rattled the walls, as did the rapid fire of fingers on keyboards. Desktops were sticky to the touch, covered in coffee-ring collages, and the air was so thick with the smell of fast food that Jonathan could almost taste the burger that Ben had eaten for lunch.

It made Jonathan feel small. The office walls were filled to bursting and seemed to have decided to squeeze back, closing in all around him. The walkways between desks were narrow and cramped, which caused clumsiness to spread like a disease, and no one was more vulnerable than Jonathan. Although tall and broad, the office had crushed and bullied him into a stooping, shuffling shadow of himself.

Even though he tried, Jonathan would still bump into people, apologise profusely, and then trudge to his desk to work as quietly as he could. It was important to Jonathan to be unnoticed. He did not want to walk tall, he did not want to stand proud, and he did not want any extra attention. Jonathan knew that unnoticed was the best thing that he could be, especially when Starcomet flashed onto the news screens.

> Finally, repeat the previous activity using the 'normal' characters developed during the activities in the last section, placed in settings of your choice. You may want to begin with the 'real' settings that you have used in previous activities from this section, then expand into local settings, and finally into 'normal' imaginary settings. The pupils will now be writing effective, multisensory locational descriptions, combining them with well-rounded characters that integrate with and affect the world around them.

SETTING PERSONIFICATION - GIVING COMIC/NARRATIVE SETTINGS THEIR OWN CHARACTER

To further improve locational writing we will introduce two literary techniques that are traditionally used, particularly in poetry, to develop settings which have a real sense of character. They are known as *pathetic fallacy* and *personification*. The pupils will, unknowingly, have begun to experiment with pathetic fallacy in the previous activities, as the technique works by suggesting that inanimate or inhuman things (e.g. objects, buildings, the weather) have feelings, thoughts or sensations imposed on them by the moods and actions of the humans in their proximity. Jonathan Steel's frenzied newsroom is a good example of the idea of a living, reactive space that mirrors the chaos of its inhabitants.

The idea of emotions 'rubbing off' on the setting will lead us into an exploration of personification, which is similar to pathetic fallacy although it does not depend on characters lending their emotions to a setting. It enables the setting to take on a character all of its own, independent from the characters that dwell within it, and critically allows it to impose its own character on to its inhabitants.

ACTIVITY 5.9: CONTAGIOUS EMOTIONS
CREATING MOOD THROUGH EXCITING LOCATIONAL DESCRIPTIONS

> Introduce the term 'pathetic fallacy' to your group and explain that a good way to give character to a setting, or to make it seem alive, is to have the living characters' emotions and actions 'rub-off' on the setting around them. Using the following example, or one of your own, demonstrate how this can be done and the effect it achieves by starting with a locational description from the previous activity then expand it using this idea of emotional rub-off:

> The gloomy, foreboding Lair was concealed deep underground like lost treasure. It housed many powerful, hi-tech computers, with dazzling screens that pierced the dark like lightning bolts. DarkSpectre trudged unhurriedly through the cave, breathing the stale air and dragging his feet across the dusty floor. He passed by rough, rocky walls that showed the scars of time, just as his battered limbs did. What little light there was seemed to shrink as he neared its source, the cave somehow sensing that he wanted nothing more than to sink into the shadows. The darkness of the cave responded, surrounding him, encasing him, wrapping him up and hiding him away from the world.

ACTIVITY 5.10: PLAYING WITH PERSONIFICATION
MAKING THE LOCATION INTO A CHARACTER

> Introduce the technique of personification by linking it to pathetic fallacy as a way of giving character to a setting. However this time those characteristics do not depend on the emotions of the people in the setting, instead they are assigned by the writer. As such, instead of exploring only how characters affect the setting, pupils will now consider how the setting also affects characters, creating a two-way interaction.

> Share the following short story about a disturbing, dangerous psychiatric hospital with your group, and while you read, ask them to imagine themselves following the narrator on a tour of the asylum.

It was supposed to be a place where people went to get better. A place of healing and wellbeing. That's what Thaddeus Darkcastle wanted when he first began building Darkcastle Asylum, but that is not how it turned out. Only a few months after the grand opening, Thaddeus became a patient and prisoner of his own hospital, driven mad by the memory of his lost family and a relentless lust for revenge. As you walk past his old, shadowy cell it calls out to you, messages scratched with fingernails into the stone wall ramble on about a 'great beast,' the 'ghost of death.'

You move further down the asylum's sprawling, murky corridors, and you begin to wonder why such a large building is so dank and poorly lit, especially as a mouse runs over your foot... at least you hope it was a mouse. The asylum used to be a proud building that depended on additional backup generators to provide enough electricity to light its many striking passageways. However, one night a patient called The Charlatan managed to convince a nurse that the man in the cell opposite him was feeling very sick and needed assistance. Unfortunately for the nurse, she was new to the job and had just started her shift, so she rushed in without checking who was in the cell. The man, if you could call him a man, was T-Bone Jackson. The other patients referred to him as 'Razor Lizard', on account of a medical condition called atavism which left him with scaled skin, immense muscles, and a powerful jaw filled with razor sharp teeth. What he did in that cell and what the doctors and nurses found in the morning meant that from then on they were glad to turn the lights as low as possible. The asylum was no longer proud, nor hungry for electricity, but had developed a taste for evil.

Arthur McTaggart, a doctor at the asylum, once accused Thaddeus Darkcastle of feeding the evil of the asylum by filling it with insane souls. Nowadays, the asylum is empty. The Charlatan led a mass escape, and now all that remains are the ghosts of the tortured patients of Darkcastle. Walk down any corridor and you can smell the fear and see the stale sweat stains on the beds of inmates sent mad by the voices of Darkcastle. You see walls marked with what you can only imagine to be the remnants of visitors to the Razor Lizard, or Stitchface, or one of the hundreds of violent visitors that have called this awful place home over the years.

Finally you reach the room at the end of the corridor. Shivering, you creep slowly and cautiously inside, one small step at a time, and suddenly you hear the steel door snap shut behind you. This is your cell. Your prison. Your home. Forever.

Welcome to Darkcastle Asylum.

Once you have finished, ask the pupils to describe their feelings and the effect the setting had on them. Explain that they have just had their own personality or 'character' affected by the character of a setting, and it is this result that they will look to emulate through their own writing. Starting with DarkSpectre, ask them to write an account of a comic character's visit to Darkcastle, focusing on combining multisensory descriptions with two-way character/setting interactions.

ACTIVITY 5.11: ALTER-EGO CONFESSIONAL
DESCRIBING REAL-WORLD SETTINGS THROUGH REAL-WORLD PERSPECTIVES

> Expand on the previous activity by replacing the comic hero with the alter ego or 'normal' character from the previous activities. Ask the pupils to write from the first person perspective. This will link to Activity 5.10 as they will again be able to put themselves 'in the shoes' of the protagonist, as well as allowing them to practise writing from different viewpoints. Suggest that this is their character's 'confessional,' an honest insight into their thoughts and feelings, and that their character should explain and be open about concerns that they might outwardly try to hide.

Your pupils will now be working to combine multisensory descriptions with two-way interactions between the character of the protagonists and the character of the setting, moving ever further into the 'real world'. The final activity will help secure transferable locational writing skills that they can apply to any setting with any character.

ACTIVITY 5.12: WHAT'S BEHIND THAT DOOR?
COMBINING LOCATIONAL DESCRIPTION TECHNIQUES

> Bring this multisensory, interactive locational writing into reality by asking the pupils to write a narrative based on a 'normal' child character who will explore the 'normal' setting of your school. However, your school isn't normal. Your school is a front, just like the X-Mansion, home to the X-Men and disguised as *Xavier's School for Gifted Youngsters*. Use pictures and if possible a movie clip from the 'X-Men' film to show how behind its walls the X-mansion contains secret training rooms, passageways and even a jet hangar hidden beneath the playground.

> Discuss with your class what secret facilities could be concealed within your school, and where they would be most likely to be hidden. Once you have brainstormed these ideas, ask your pupils to complete the exploration narrative, written from either the first or third person perspective, and focused on multisensory descriptions and interactions that affect both character and setting.

CHAPTER 6
DEVELOPING
PUNCTUATION, GRAMMAR, VOCABULARY & SPELLING
THROUGH COMICS

TEACHING THE ACCURATE USE OF PUNCTUATION THROUGH COMICS

Punctuation is an integral part of writing composition. It affects meaning, clarifies information, and enables the reader to decode a text efficiently. It is also a complicated, often perplexingly subtle and, at times, subjective skill that would require more than a chapter to explore in its entirety.

Therefore, this chapter will not focus on the 'basics' of punctuation (e.g. where to place a capital letter). Instead, it will build upon the foundations laid in Alan Peat's *Get Your Head Around Punctuation (...and how to teach it!)*, as well as pupils' pre-existing punctuation knowledge, to develop and improve their use of a variety of punctuation marks.

ACTIVITY 6.1: LET'S TALK SPEECH
DEVELOPING DIALOGUE WORK

We will start by focusing on written dialogue, where punctuation can be particularly tricky. Comics are an extremely useful resource for developing an understanding of written speech.

Comic speech bubbles can be used to teach the correct use of speech marks. We will expand upon this to form a complex, comic-based dialogue through which different types of punctuation may be practised. In addition, we will explore various phrase and clause types that might be included to enhance written dialogue.

METHOD

> Select a single comic cell, preferably containing only two speaking characters, and blank out the speech thus:

> Discuss with the pupils what the characters might be saying. This is where the comic form proves particularly useful, as you can draw pupils' attention to body language, gestures and facial expressions, encouraging them to infer dialogue from a broad range of visual clues. Select the most effective suggestions and use them to fill the speech bubbles:

> Now model how the contents of the bubbles become the speech in written dialogue by surrounding them with speech marks, then adding a speaking verb and a speaker, e.g.

"I thought I heard you sneaking around," **said DarkSpectre.**

"I didn't want to interrupt. Who's this," **said Blastboy.**

Draw the pupils' attention to the fact that some punctuation is included **inside the speech** marks to fully communicate the meaning of the speech. Adopt the 'mantle of the fool' (the use of deliberate errors as a teaching strategy) and tell them you think you might have made a punctuation mistake. Once the missing question mark has been identified, show that it must be including **inside** the speech marks, as it is part of the character's speech (e.g. it makes it clear that they are **questioning** the other character).

> Once the idea of 'speech marks replacing speech bubbles' has been grasped, provide pupils with a full page of comic action in which all the speech is blanked out. (You could retain some speech or add in your own sentence starters to support learners of different abilities.) It may look something like this:

> Repeat the input for the whole page, allowing an extended dialogue to develop. The completed page may look like this:

> Use this extended dialogue to begin a discussion about speaking verbs, considering alternatives to overused words such as 'said'. Ask the pupils to predict the character's mood, and then let those suggestions guide their contributions, modelling an example with a variety of verbs to help. Remember to draw attention to the necessary **punctuation**, both inside and outside the speech marks:

"I thought I heard you sneaking around," said DarkSpectre.

sighed DarkSpectre.

moaned DarkSpectre.

grumbled DarkSpectre.

muttered DarkSpectre.

> Move on to consider the second character's reply; ask the pupils to think about how the character reacted to what he was told. Discuss how the character might have felt as he replied, focusing on specific emotions. Use this opportunity to again practise the correct formatting of dialogue punctuation, as well as the use of an exciting speech verb, followed by the introduction of the speaking adverb. As a group, indentify an emotional state as a root word (e.g. curious,) then discuss ways to turn it into an adverb (in this case by adding the 'ly' suffix,) then model the correct recording of their suggestions, e.g.:

"I didn't want to interrupt. Who's this?" asked Blastboy curiously.

enthusiastically.

nosily.

inquisitively.

quietly.

shyly.

> For the third line of dialogue, ask the pupils to identify an emotion that the speaker might be experiencing as he talks. However, this time you want them to 'show not tell' the emotion. In other words, think of a character action that would suggest his emotion. If necessary, pop on your Oscar-winning actor hat and dramatise some emotional actions for the pupils to guess. Start basic (smile/frown) then mime more complex emotions (gritted teeth / bowed head / shaking fist / tapping toe / rolling eyes / intense stare etc.) Ask the pupils to guess your emotions and then look again at the comic to infer the character's emotions. Use the suggestions to model a short description to add to the speech, e.g.

"Not sure yet. I need to do more tests," DarkSpectre replied dismissively, shrugging his shoulders.

"Not sure yet. I need to do more tests," DarkSpectre replied dismissively, narrowing his eyes and glaring at the screen.

"Not sure yet. I need to do more tests," DarkSpectre replied dismissively, avoiding Blastboy's eyes.

"Not sure yet. I need to do more tests," DarkSpectre replied dismissively, tapping the luminous screen whilst he awaited the results.

In this example, draw the pupils' attention to the **comma** used to separate the 'show not tell' verb from the speaking adverb, another crucial use of effective punctuation.

> Finally, use inference to develop the description of location. Ask the pupils to identify, in the comic cell containing the next line of speech, something which might be occurring in the background. Assure them that this answer can come as much from their imagination as from what they can see, as long as it is appropriate and makes sense in the context of the narrative. Offer extra rewards if they can find something that will reflect the 'mood' of the speech as it is developing (e.g. if the characters are angry with one another, is there anything occurring which might add to the general atmosphere of anger?) Model an example:

"Can I help out?" Blastboy requested hopefully as a lonely, chilling wind whistled through the lab.

"Can I help out?" Blastboy requested hopefully as yet another error message popped up on the screen.

"Can I help out?" Blastboy requested hopefully as expensive machines whirred and hummed softly all around him.

"Can I help out?" Blastboy requested hopefully as the narrow light lit up his eager face.

> As a final extension, provide the pupils with a new comic strip with blank dialogue bubbles. Remind them of the basics of recording speech:

...the contents of the bubbles, including punctuation, go inside the speech marks, and nothing else!

and of the effective speech tools they have been practising:

...use exciting speaking verbs and adverbs...

...use 'show not tell'...

...use 'as adverbials!'

Ask pupils to complete the comic strip and then use it, along with their accurate speech punctuation and speech-enhancing-techniques, to create a full written dialogue. As an extension/differentiated activity you might ask the pupils to create a dialogue with a specific mood, e.g. produce a dialogue which expresses happiness/frustration/enmity/co-operation. As the pupils become more comfortable with this process, you can begin to remove the comic strip support (for those who need more support, a comic 'starter' might be appropriate).

Once the pupils are confident in their use of dialogue, they can move on to characters from your genre of choice.

ACTIVITY 6.2: YOU CANNOT BE SERIOUS?
USING THE QUESTION MARK FOR DOUBT

The question mark is a multifaceted punctuation mark that may be used to indicate a query or to demonstrate uncertainty in a statement, whilst the exclamation mark can be used in different ways, including the indication of intense emotions. Again, the fundamental applications of both of these marks are covered in the aforementioned book, and it is probable that many pupils will have grasped concepts such as, 'a question needs a question mark at the end,' and 'an exclamation mark comes after something loud'. So to avoid repetition we will focus on a more advanced use of question marks and exclamation marks to improve descriptions and enhance characters' internal and external dialogue.

METHOD

> One engaging, yet often overlooked, use of the question mark is to demonstrate doubt in a character's mind over something they have discovered. Share the image below:

> Discuss with the pupils what it is that turns this speech into a question. Together you will identify the 'can it?' phrase, which will allow you to introduce the 'question mark for doubt'. Model how the speech consists of two parts, the **statement** and the **tag question**, and use the opportunity to review the correct formatting of recorded speech with the necessary punctuation as you go:

"This can't be real, can it?" questioned Strikeback angrily.

Statement   Tag question

> Explain that adding the tag question suggests that the character is uncertain about, or refuses to believe, what he sees or thinks, and that this adds both an engaging vulnerability to his character and an extra layer of excitement to the action. Challenge the pupils to come up with appropriate tag questions for the following statements:

"Strikeback will save those children,....................?"

"That shield isn't strong enough,...........................?"

"Starcomet can't lift that whole building,.........................?"

"The mutants don't understand us,.......................?"

> Through this exercise it should become clear that the tag question begins with a word from the first half of the sentence, which is now inverted (i.e. 'will' becomes 'won't', 'can't' becomes 'can' and so on). After having secured this idea, provide the pupils with the following comic cells which they can fill in with a statement of opinion or observation (drawn from something surprising which is happening in the picture) and the tag question (using the inverted word) to create their own 'question mark for doubt' dialogue:

> Once the pupils have grasped the idea of how to create 'question mark for doubt' dialogue, ask them to go back to the speech work from Activity 6.1 and rework or extend it to include this new feature. This will enable them to practise formatting and situating this feature correctly.

> Extend the use of the 'question mark for doubt' by substituting the speech bubble for a thought bubble, like so:

> Ask the pupils whether the contents of the thought bubble would need speech marks if they were to write it down. Agree that although these are the character's thoughts, he is still speaking, if only to himself. Therefore, if we wish to include a character's thoughts, they too require accurate use of punctuation:

"This can't be real, can it?" wondered Strikeback angrily.

> Draw the pupils' attention to the altered speech verb, and ask them to compare it with the original speech.

127

Ask them why they think it needed changing. Agree that the new verb 'wondered' makes it clear that this speech is taking place inside Strikeback's mind. Once this idea is established, ask the pupils to use the pictures from the last part of the activity and create their own internal 'question mark for doubt' speech examples, including accurately placed punctuation and an appropriate speaking verb. Again, this can be included in their expanded dialogue writing once they feel confident enough.

> As an extension, ask the pupils to think about some internal speech that adds to the emotional complexity of the character by showing self-doubt – questioning their own actions with words like should/could/would, e.g.

"I shouldn't have done that, should I?" Strikeback thought to himself.

"I couldn't have done any more for him, could I?" Roborg wondered desperately.

"Blastboy wouldn't betray me, would he?" DarkSpectre hoped desperately.

Delving into the thoughts of the protagonist in this way and demonstrating control of an internal, psychological narrative will not only engage the reader, but will show excellent authorial manipulation in other fictional genres.

ACTIVITY 6.3: EXCLAMATION STATIONS

In this section we will consider how to extend the use of exclamation marks. The first technique we will look at involves using the exclamation mark to demonstrate a character's surprise through repetition, as in the examples below,

"I can pick up a double-decker bus, one-handed," Starcomet boasted proudly. "Wow – a double-decker bus!" the surprised boy replied.

METHOD

> Show the class this example and ask them to explain what is happening. Agree that the character is repeating something that they can't quite believe, perhaps to check if they heard it correctly, and the exclamation mark demonstrates their surprise. To expand this technique, show how adding a short descriptive sentence conclusion can help the reader better understand the emotion of the speaker:

"I can pick up a double-decker bus, one-handed." Starcomet boasted proudly. "Wow – a double-decker bus!" the surprised boy replied. His dad was a bus driver so he knew exactly how heavy a double-decker was.

> Provide the pupils with the following comic starters and, using the comic character of their choice, have them follow your example and complete the repeated exclamation speech and the explanation. If necessary, support them in choosing the correct part to repeat, and model accurate embedded punctuation.

1. "I'm sorry. Your parents are dead," admitted Geeves reluctantly.
2. "I quit," announced Blastboy confidently.
3. "I have a secret; I am actually your father," Steve revealed quietly.
4. "Shapeshifter can take on any shape he wants," Captain Z cautioned.
5. "It's my birthday today. I'm 123 years old," the Stellar Warrior declared joyfully.

> Again, once the pupils use this new technique confidently, ask them to include it in their developing long dialogue work. As an extension activity, you might wish to consider how to use brackets for the explanation statement, e.g.

"I can pick up a double-decker bus, one-handed," Starcomet boasted proudly. "A double-decker bus!" the surprised boy replied (his dad was a bus driver so he knew exactly how heavy a double-decker was).

This will allow you to develop the idea of surrounding authorial intrusions with brackets, (Authorial intrusion: where the author interrupts to provide some extra detail or opinions not volunteered by, or clear from, the characters alone.)

> The linking of onomatopoeia and exclamation marks is also easily taught through comics, which not only feature many familiar onomatopoeic words attached directly to an action, (remember the 1960's Batman TV series; Sock! Bang! Crash! etc,) they also contain useful examples of neologisms, e.g.:

> Tell the pupils that they are going to play a game with three main players, though anyone in the class can jump in and steal points. Provide a comic stimulus which contains a clear action –

> Explain that the challenge for Player One is to generate a sensible onomatopoeic suggestion that describes the sound of the action. Player Two must then attempt to phonetically spell the sound, including a final exclamation mark to indicate energy/emotion. Player Three must then take the word and use it to commence a description of the action. Model the process in the following way:

Player 1: *Makes a whooshing sound, with a little fizz to indicate energy*
Player 2: *Spells*   Woo-sheesh!
Player 3: *Writes*   Woo-sheesh! Lightning Boy blasted through the police tape like a flash, then stopped to examine the crime scene.

> As the pupils become more adept at creating and explaining their own sensible onomatopoeic terms, including the exclamation mark for emphasis, challenge them to include some examples in their own dialogue, perhaps as a result of/precursor to some questioning/exclamation dialogue.

ACTIVITY 6.4: COMMA CONFUSION
SEPARATING SPEECH TO ADD TENSION

The comma can be one of the most challenging punctuation marks to teach, mostly because its expanded use is often based on a context-dependent or stylistic decision, rather than a steadfast rule. However, using the original dialogue from Activity 6.1, we might find a way to employ the comma to demonstrate a masterful control of speech punctuation through a fairly simple technique.

METHOD

> Revisit the following line from the original dialogue as a class:

> **"I thought I heard you sneaking around," barked DarkSpectre.**

> Then display the following version:

> **"I thought I heard you," DarkSpectre barked, "sneaking around."**

> Ask the pupils what has changed. Once they have identified the positional shift of the speaker/speech verb phrase, ask them what effect this creates. Agree together that moving the phrase, using some carefully placed commas, gives the impression that DarkSpectre pauses before he says "sneaking around." This makes him sound suspicious, perhaps even hinting at mistrust. Make it clear that the speaker/speaking verb phrase **does not** go inside speech marks, as the character does not say these words, hence the speech marks closing and re-opening around what he **does say** (revisit the speech bubble work to review this idea if necessary).

> Model the following examples and explore how they should be changed to add a dramatic pause to the speech:

Q1. "Sorry Blastboy, this is top secret," DarkSpectre apologised as he continued his work.

A1. "Sorry Blastboy," DarkSpectre apologised as he continued his work, "this is top secret."

Q2. "Not sure yet, I need to do more tests," DarkSpectre admitted with uncertainty.

A2. "Not sure yet," DarkSpectre admitted with uncertainty, "I need to do more tests."

Q3. "I don't know who I can trust right now..." DarkSpectre mumbled cryptically.

A3. "I don't know who I can trust," DarkSpectre mumbled cryptically, "right now..."

> Once pupils are comfortable splitting speech this way, ask them to introduce some examples into their ongoing dialogue work. As an extension, you may introduce the idea of **beginning** the dialogue with the speaker/speaking verb/comma phrase, e.g.

DarkSpectre mumbled cryptically, "I don't know who I can trust right now..."

> Additionally, use the opportunity to develop the use of the subordinate clause (or 'sandwich sentence,' or 'Noun/who/which/where sentence,') e.g.

DarkSpectre, who was caught up in his research, mumbled cryptically, "I don't know who I can trust right now..."

Blastboy, who was always looking for the opportunity to impress, asked hopefully, "Can I help out?"

Blastboy, who was in a state of shock, demanded angrily, "I thought you trusted me, partner?"

> Again, once understood, ask the pupils to include this technique in their own dialogue.

133

ACTIVITY 6.5: APOSTROPHE THE THIEF
USING APOSTROPHES FOR OMISSION

The apostrophe can be used to mark possession or omission. The use of the apostrophe for possession is a fairly simple concept, and one dealt with clearly and concisely in Alan Peat's *Get Your Head Around Punctuation*, although comic examples do make it fun to explore:

The indestructible swords belonging to Blastboy =

Blastboy's indestructible swords

The luminous, powerful shield belonging to Cosmic Soldier =

Cosmic Soldier's luminous, powerful shield

The weaponized tank belonging to the Z-Men =

The Z-Men's weaponized tank

The gadgets belonging to DarkSpectre =

DarkSpectre's gadgets

However, as we are looking predominantly at speech, the apostrophe for omission may provide a more prescient focus. In terms of expressing characteristics and personality through dialogue, the avoidance or inclusion of the apostrophe for omission might help us to demonstrate a character's formal or informal nature.

For example, the highly educated Captain Z from the Z-Men might say:

"We shall not join forces with Magmaman when it is abundantly clear that he is hell bent on war. We cannot possibly entertain the idea, and we should not encourage those who do."

Yet the rough and ready, blue-collar Saberwolf might say:

"I ain't gonna join with those goons, no chance. Magnaman's a fool, he's a certified wacko, and I wouldn't go near him with a ten-foot cattle prod. You've got nothing to worry about from me, boss."

METHOD

> After displaying and discussing these examples, provide pupils with the following dialogue, and tell them that the character's speech has been mixed up. Ask them to change the contractions to their expanded form to make Captain Z sound more formal, as well as using the apostrophe for contraction as much as possible to show Saberwolf's more informal character:

Captain Z, who was the leader of the Z-men, addressed his team. "We won't join forces with Magnaman when it's abundantly clear that he's hell bent on war. We can't possibly entertain the idea, and we shouldn't encourage those who do."

"I am not going to join with those goons, no chance. Magnaman is a fool, he is a certified wacko, and I would not go near him with a ten-foot cattle prod. You have got nothing to worry about from me, boss," Saberwolf assured Captain Z with a knowing wink.

"Thanks, Saberwolf," Captain Z replied. "I know you're a sensible man, and you know who to trust. I haven't known any mutant more dangerous than Magnaman, and I'm sure you won't underestimate him."

Saberwolf, who had come up against Magnaman before, agreed, "Will not happen, boss, and I will make sure we have plenty of people on the lookout for trouble."

> Once this exercise has been completed, ask the pupils to revisit the dialogue they wrote for Activity 6.1 and, using their character knowledge and inferential skills, decide which character would be the more/less formal (perhaps the older, wiser and well brought-up DarkSpectre would likely be more formal in character than the younger, street-raised Blastboy.) Ask them to modify their speech accordingly, either including or avoiding the apostrophe for omission to suit.

ACTIVITY 6.6: JUST ONE MORE THING...
USING ELLIPSIS TO CONVEY UNCERTAINTY

During 'Activity 3.11: A Trip Down Memory Lane' from Chapter 3 (p73), we explored the use of ellipsis [...] to indicate a missing period of time in the transition between flashback and present narrative time frames. Now we will consider ways in which the ellipsis mark can be integrated into dialogue for dramatic effect.

Take the expanded line from the dialogue example in Activity 6.1:

DarkSpectre, who was caught up in his research, mumbled cryptically, "I don't know who I can trust right now..."

METHOD

> Share the following examples and, for each, discuss what could be on the character's mind:

"The answer is out there somewhere," Strikeback whispered. "I'm sure of it..."

"I believe you..." Cosmic Soldier stated deviously.

"We won't be hearing from him...for a long time," Starcomet declared.

> Ensure that the punctuation rules for using the ellipsis mark are made clear as you discuss these examples; the three dots are part of the speech, thus are contained inside the speech marks.

> Ask the pupils again to revisit their dialogue work and see if they can make any sentences shorter by using the ellipsis mark to suggest uncertainty. Encourage them to use the example we have shared, and then ask them to expand their dialogue further to include their own, following the modelled examples.

> The ellipsis also works to add a longer pause than a full stop, which can create tension in speech. Show the pupils this example from the expanded dialogue:

> | Blastboy, who was in a state of shock, demanded angrily, "I thought you trusted me, partner?"

> Discuss the effects of replacing the comma in this speech with an ellipsis:

> | Blastboy, who was in a state of shock, demanded angrily, "I thought you trusted me... partner?"

> Explain that this longer pause indicates an element of doubt: is DarkSpectre really trustworthy? Provide the pupils with the following examples and ask them to identify where the ellipsis could be used to create tension:

> | The Stellar Warrior announced confidently, "I know you are in here, Magnaman, somewhere."
>
> "I've finally got it, the key to eternal life," Dr Devious announced with delirious laughter.
>
> The Charlatan who had been quieter than usual, finally spoke, "I've got a plan. They won't know what's hit them."

> Again, make sure the punctuation rules for using ellipsis are clarified as you explore these examples. Ask pupils to see if they can add tension to their dialogue work by using the ellipsis mark as appropriate, following your modelled examples.

Through activities 6.1 - 6.6, pupils will have gained knowledge and experience of the correct formatting of recorded speech, with the inclusion of descriptive phrases drawn from settings and characters that engage the reader and embellish the dialogue. They will be able to use questioning skilfully to introduce doubt and disbelief into their character's internal and external speech. They will also be able to use exclamation marks to express a wide range of reactive emotions, as well as pairing them with innovative onomatopoeic terms that demonstrate writing flair, intensified by the use of commas for embedded clauses. They will use apostrophes to increase or decrease levels of formality in their characters as they see fit, and they will use the ellipsis mark to create tension. All these skills, developed through comics, will easily transfer to any genre of writing. Who said punctuation had to be boring...?

IMPROVING NARRATIVE: EFFECTIVE EDITING AT WORD AND SENTENCE LEVEL

Improving grammar (i.e. the selection, formation and placement of correct vocabulary) and accurate spelling are both essential to crafting an engaging narrative. We cannot expect pupils to develop an expansive vocabulary, nor develop complex spelling techniques, entirely by themselves. Again, comics can help greatly. They are accessible and undoubtedly encourage reluctant readers, (for more on this, see Chapter 2). Their vocabulary is as complex and rich as any other comparative genres, like novels or short stories.

If we want to help pupils develop a rich vocabulary and a confident control of the written word, they need direct, focused input. This does not mean that vocabulary and spelling practice need be delivered in the form of monotonous, decontextualised tests or worksheets. What follows is a selection of games and competitive activities, not unlike mental maths starters, which will help pupils to develop grammar, vocabulary and spelling skills that they will apply during later activities in the chapter.

ACTIVITY 6.7: LET BATTLE COMMENCE!
GAMES TO IMPROVE SPELLING AND VOCABULARY

> *Game 1: Vocabulary Battles*

This is a three-player game, but can involve the whole class if you wish. It is not unlike the onomatopoeic activity from the previous section: Player One is responsible for generating a word, (past-tense verbs and exciting adjectives both work well). Player Two is responsible for spelling the word, and Player Three for using it in a descriptive sentence. However, if you provide the rest of the class with whiteboards, they can all be involved, as they write their own suggestions for each stage of the game so that you might call on their ideas if any of the players 'get stuck' or suggest an incorrect or inappropriate answer. In terms of developing vocabulary, you may choose to change the task of Player Three to that of 'defining the word,' specifying that they must avoid using the word they are defining in the definition, and must avoid use of the word 'you.' Model the game with the following examples:

Teacher: Round 1, a past tense verb please!
Player One: Manipulated
Player Two: M-a-n-i-p-u-l-a-t-e-d
Player Three: To have influenced or controlled someone's behaviour.

Or

Teacher: Round 2, an exciting adjective please!
Player One: Dense
Player Two: D-e-n-c-e
Teacher: Not quite! Can anyone steal the points?
(Child holds up whiteboard and spells correctly.)
Teacher: Correct! And the definition?
Player Three: Thick and not easy to get through.

To add a comic-based element, suggest that Player One, whoever they may be, is fighting for the Avengers, Player Two for the X-Men, and Player Three for the Justice League. The teams can then amass points over the course of a half-term.

> *Game 2: Register Rally*

A quick word exercise to start the day. The register rally works particularly well if the pupils have time to read prior to the register being taken. Ask them to think of/find an exciting word (specify the type; verbs and adjectives work well). Even if they are unfamiliar with it, ask them to try to vocalise it. As you take the register, the pupils reply with their word for the day. You can then choose effective or interesting words and check their definitions. The pupil could, again, win points for their 'comic team' if they can put together an accurate definition. If they cannot, another child may step in and offer a definition, potentially earning bonus points for their team. If no one is able to define the word, the teacher could 'step in'. You will notice that, as the pupils become used to the process, the register speeds up (as the pupils arrive with words prepared – evidence that they are independently increasing their vocabulary), the suggested words increase in complexity cand effectiveness, and begin creeping into their written work.

> Game 3: Spelling Crunch

Arrange the pupils in a circle then select a comic you have been using in class and an exciting descriptive/action word. Challenge the pupils and offer one letter each (in sequence around the circle) in order to complete the spelling of the word. If any child suggests an incorrect letter or hesitates, they must sit down, and the word starts again from the next child until it is completed, at which point the 'full stop fella' (the next child) has to sit down. Repeat this with a variety of vocabulary until there are two players left, then set them head-to-head with a word of your choice. The winner earns points for their comic team. To extend the challenge of the game (other than obviously increasing the complexity of the spellings), introduce the commands 'reverse' and 'backwards'. When the 'reverse' command is given, the direction of play changes on that letter, so clockwise movement through the players becomes anti-clockwise from the same point. When the 'backwards' command is given, the play continues in the same direction, but the word is spelled backwards from the current letter, for example:

Teacher: The spelling word is 'Horrific.'

Player One: H

Player Two: o

Player Three: r

Player Four: r

Player Five: i

Teacher: Backwards!

Player Six: r

Player Seven: r

Player Eight: o

Player Nine: H

Teacher: Correct! And the full stop fella sits down!

> Game 4: Verb/Adverb Charades

This is a game which combines body-language drama with grammar development. Provide each pupil with a whiteboard, and suggest the name of a comic hero to the class. Model a Noun/Verb/Adverb phrase for them, on the board, which includes this character, for example:

Amazon wept uncontrollably.

Following your modelled example, have each pupil write a Noun/Verb/Adverb example on their boards. Suggest that you will pick the most original, creative and exciting examples. Once they have finished, ask them to show their boards. Select one in your head, and then ask all the pupils to clear their boards. Write the example you have chosen on your own whiteboard, then pick two volunteers and ask them to come to the front. Show them the board and challenge them to act out the Noun/Verb/Adverb example. It is now the rest of the class's job to infer the Noun/Verb/Adverb clause from their actions. Once they have had enough time to complete the task, ask them all to show their boards. If anyone has exactly the correct wording, they win points for their comic team. However, the other pupils' writing will provide an opportunity to praise and reward alternative suggestions which also include effective vocabulary.

> ## Game 5: Vocabulary Combat

As a physical extension of the Verb/Adverb charades, select two combatants of similar ability to compete against each other. Assign each of these pupils a comic character, and have them take turns to score either a 2 hit (Noun+Verb), 3 hit (Noun+Verb+Adverb), or a 4 hit (Noun+Verb+Adverb+As adverbial) verbal combination. If the pupil falters or uses an inappropriate/incorrect term, they forfeit their attack. The first player to 10 points scores a victory for their team. Model the following combat as an example:

Teacher: Players Ready? Commence Vocabulary Combat!
Player 1: Roborg smashed.
Teacher: 2 hits!
Player 2: Strikeback swung gracefully.
Teacher: 3 hits!
Player 1: Roborg roared angrily.
Teacher: 3 hits!
Player 2: Strikeback dashed speedily as his enemy gained on him.
Teacher: 4 hits!
etc...

> ## Game 6: Countdown to Chaos

Display a selection of comic character names and provide each pupil with a whiteboard and pen. Use the display as part of a 'Countdown' style game, in which the pupils use letters from the character names to generate and correctly spell the longest word they possibly can in one minute. This activity is easily differentiated, in that you can limit higher ability pupils to using, for example, only two of the four available names, and ban them from repeating letters (i.e. if there is one 'T' on the board it can only be used once) or suggesting words with fewer than five letters. By the same token, the less able learners may repeat letters, use all the available names, and suggest words of any length. Make correct spelling the primary focus of this activity, and award points to the comic teams of players who suggest the longest correctly spelt words from each ability group.

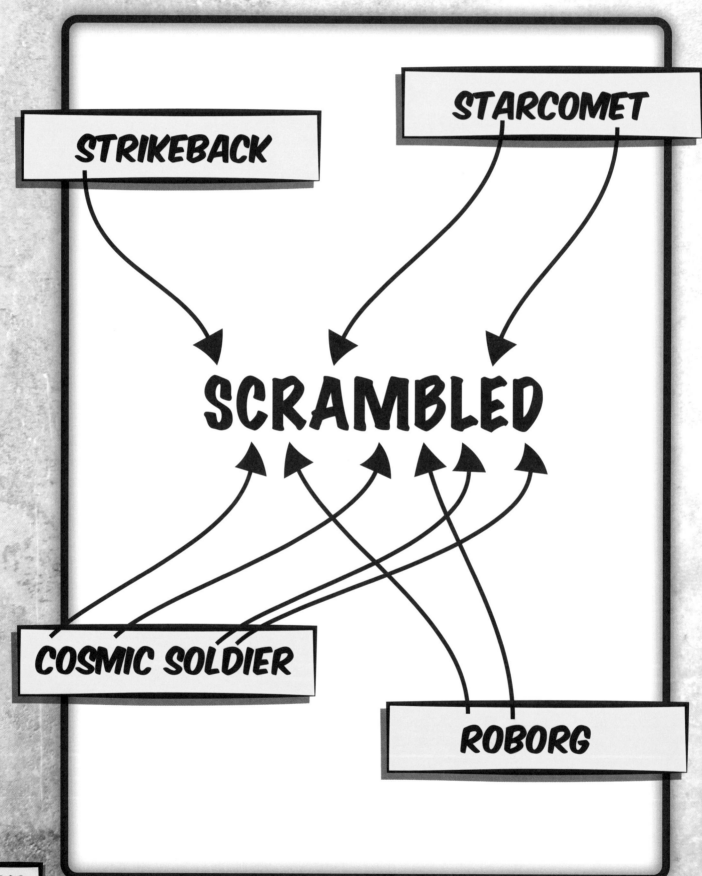

ACTIVITY 6.8: BORING MADE BETTER
DEVELOPING EDITING SKILLS

Whilst the above games and activities are enjoyable, they are of limited value if we do not ensure that the skills are applied! The following activities will demonstrate ways that pupils might employ their improved vocabulary and spelling as part of an editing process, starting with word-level work.

METHOD

> Display the following 'dull' sentence.

Thor hit the boulder.

> Agree that whilst this sentence gives a clear idea of what is happening, the writer has missed some great vocabulary opportunities which we must take advantage of. Firstly, replace 'boring' words. The pupils should feel more confident to suggest exciting past tense verbs following their vocabulary games, so start there. Ask for a selection of alternatives to 'hit', the more the better!

Thor smashed the boulder.

destroyed

struck

demolished

hammered

pounded

clobbered

> Refer back to the speaking verb/adverb work from Activity 6.7 in the first section of this chapter, and suggest that we might also be able to include an adverb here, this time at the end of the phrase. Ask the pupils how, or in what manner, the character is carrying out the action, getting them to identify an emotional state. Then using their spelling knowledge, ask them to turn it into an adverb. Again, take as wide a selection of ideas as you can. If a pupil suggests an inappropriate term, take the time to ask the class to decide why it is inappropriate, which in itself will help them to develop their selective vocabulary further.

Thor smashed the boulder violently.

aggressively.

ferociously.

viciously.

forcefully.

fiercely.

brutally.

> Next, shift the focus to the object in the sentence (in this case, the boulder). Explain that another descriptive opportunity has been missed here, and that we could include a short adjective list to describe the boulder. Brainstorm suggestions for adjectives before selecting the two most effective ones. This will not only demonstrate how selective judgement of appropriate vocabulary is an important skill in itself, but will also provide a teaching opportunity regarding the accurate placement of the comma in the list:

Thor smashed the vast, jagged boulder violently.

pointy

rough

solid

mottled

ancient

> Finally, refer the class back to the 'as adverbial' clauses used in the dialogue work at the end of Activity 6.7. Ask the pupils to use their imagination and think of something else that could be going on at the same time as the action. Offer extra points for suggestions that add to the mood that was identified when they generated the adverb (in this case, violence and conflict.) If necessary, model an example to prompt the pupils:

Thor smashed the vast, jagged boulder violently as his frightened enemies cowered behind it.

> Again, hear a selection of ideas before selecting and recording the one which enhances the mood of the sentence most effectively. Finally, compare the original phrase –

Thor hit the boulder.

– directly with the new phrase compiled by the class, e.g.

Thor smashed the vast, jagged boulder violently as his frightened enemies cowered behind it.

> The striking difference between the two sentences, coupled with the exciting comic stimulus, will encourage the pupils and boost their editing confidence. Applying the modelled example, provide pupils with a range of boring sentences (below) and ask them to go through the same editing process to improve them as much as possible.

Strikeback saved the baby.

DarkSpectre threw the thug.

Amazon hurt the monster.

Roborg saved the soldiers.

> As the pupils become accustomed to the process of finding and fixing missed language opportunities in comic examples, change the 'boring sentences' to make them reflect the conventions and content of the text type you are studying. Subsequently, ask them to go through this same editing process when they finish their own narrative writing.

ACTIVITY 6.9: CHANGE FOR THE BETTER
EXTENDING EDITING SKILLS

When editing a narrative it becomes clear that sometimes, instead of single word adjustments or additions, an entire phrase may need to be substituted or incorporated to improve a sentence. This activity considers 'whole phrase' changes via questioning.

METHOD

> Display the following description, made up of three 'boring' sentences, not unlike those from Activity 6.8:

Thor stood on the hill. He grabbed his hammer. He threw it.

> *Before* introducing 'whole phrase' editing, recap learning from the previous activity. Hopefully, by using vocabulary switching, adding adverbs and adjectives, and perhaps including an adverbial clause, you might get something like this:

Thor positioned himself confidently on the lofty, steep hill. He viciously snatched up his hammer. He threw it as his enemies scattered across the fields below.

> Explain that whilst this is a great sentence, if we were to follow the same pattern for every sentence we edited, the effect would be lost and writing would become repetitive. Instead, we will now consider how we might add new, whole clauses to improve writing. Show the first short sentence:

Thor stood on the hill.

> Ask the pupils, **what could Thor be doing whilst he was standing on the hill?** Remind them that they will earn extra points if they come up with an action that adds mood to the sentence. Take the most effective suggestion and use it to model the insertion of a subordinate clause that describes an emotion-driven action, reminding them that they have already used these in their dialogue work, e.g.

Thor, who was shaking with rage, stood on the hill.

Thor, who was almost exhausted, stood on the hill.

Thor, who had finally caught up with his foe, stood on the hill.

> Having successfully edited the first short sentence, display the next one:

He grabbed his hammer.

> This time change the question to _How did Thor grab his hammer?_ Tell the pupils you are looking for an adverb, most likely ending in 'ly', which adds to the mood they created in the first short sentence. Remind them that they have already added these descriptive terms to verbs in the previous activity. This time, however, they will **start** the sentence with the adverb! Use their suggestions to model an example of how this works. You can also point out the use of the comma after the adverb to consolidate accurate use of punctuation.

> Anxiously, he grabbed his hammer.

> Viciously, he grabbed his hammer.

> Bravely, he grabbed his hammer.

> Explain that by placing the adverb at the start of the sentence the pupils are avoiding the repetitive pattern of beginning each sentence with a noun/pronoun. Varying sentence openers is a feature of higher level writing, and yet, following a process like this, it is relatively simple to accomplish. Finally, display the last short sentence:

> He threw it.

> Change the question again, this time to _What was Thor doing at the same time as throwing the hammer?_ Stipulate that this time the phrase cannot start with 'as.' Model the following examples to make it clear what you are aiming for:

> With a mighty roar, he threw it.

> Gathering his strength, he threw it.

> Taking aim at his enemy, he threw it.

> With a final swing, he threw it.

> With a gasp of effort, he threw it.

> Once the pupils grasp the idea and provide you with a selection of appropriate examples, combine this final sentence with the examples and compare the original,

> Thor stood on the hill. He grabbed his hammer. He threw it.

> with their new and improved sentence:

> Thor, who was shaking with rage, stood on the hill. Anxiously, he grabbed his hammer. Gathering his strength, he threw it.

> Again, the remarkable difference between the two sets of sentences should increase the pupil's editing confidence. Now provide the pupils with a range of similar short, 'boring', comic-based sentences (such as those below) and ask them to complete the process to improve them.

DarkSpectre climbed into the SpectreRacer. He started the engine. He drove away.

(Example edit :) DarkSpectre, who was tired and bruised, climbed into the SpectreRacer. Hesitantly, he started the engine. With a grimace, he drove away.

Strikeback jumped onto the roof. He pulled on his mask. He jumped off the building.

Starcomet woke up. He heard screaming. He jumped up and flew out.

The Stellar Warrior climbed out of the tank. He spotted his friends. He rushed towards them.

> As the pupils become more adept at finding opportunities to extend ineffective phrases, change the example to reflect the style of your current studied text type. Extend this further by asking them to apply this process to their independent work.

Saberwolf walked into the forest. He looked around. He moved forward.

Saberwolf, sensing his enemy, walked into the forest. Nervously he looked around. Spotting his enemy, he moved forward.

Thor stood on the hill. He grabbed his hammer. He threw it.

Thor, who was bruised, stood on the hill. Breathlessly he grabbed his hammer. With a final gasp, he threw it.

By Kevin, aged 10

ACTIVITY 6.10: DECODE THE DOCUMENT
CORRECTING ERRORS AND APPLYING EDITING SKILLS

Having established the notion that developing vocabulary and spelling skills through games is only really useful if the new knowledge is applied in some way, we subsequently considered a number of ways that pupils might employ an expanded vocabulary to improve work. In this activity we will apply the same process to the development of spelling skills.

METHOD

> Tell the pupils that their favourite comic team (e.g. The Avengers, The Justice League etc.) has sent them a secret document. They have heard that the class has been working to improve its spelling and grammar skills, and need the pupils' help in decoding the message. There are so many mistakes that their computer cannot make sense of it, and there are no language specialists amongst the scientists in their team. Show them the following document:

```
the device what you's are lucking four is
hiddened in side a towers ontop of the
tallist summit in the midwest the
combeenashion 4 the lok is too ate won for
free.to deeactiv ate a deviceyou must
attat-ch a mag net to the metal pins  on
the side and pul them in slowly Gud luk!
```

> Select and highlight phrases from the text, then ask members of the class to attempt to read them. After establishing that, in its current form, the text is hard to understand, ask if any of the pupils can suggest corrections that might help to make sense of the document. Specify that only suggestions which include full explanations of what is incorrect and how it can be corrected will be accepted. Model the following correctly formatted answers if necessary:

A sentence must start with a capital letter, and the first word of the paragraph is missing a capital 'T.' It should be spelled capital T-h-e.

In what should be the second sentence the writer has used the incorrect homophone 'four,' which is to do with numbers. The correct form and spelling of the word is f-o-r.

> Once the pupils get the idea of locating, explaining and correcting the errors, tell them that they have been asked to write an official report about the secret document. Provide them with their own copy of the text to annotate. Ask them to number each error they find, and then write the number in their books with an explanation of the mistake and a remedial solution. This will ensure that they will not only spot and correct errors, but will think carefully about what exactly caused the problem, and the specific spelling rule or method they are going to use to fix it.

> Extend this activity by providing alternate texts in which the errors are less obvious. You could even tailor the texts to include errors which the pupils commonly make, thereby personalising it. Follow this by changing the text type to suit your chosen genre, and, most importantly set this as an editing extension task when pupils finish their own work.

ACTIVITY 6.11: TYING IT ALL TOGETHER
APPLYING PUNCTUATION, SPELLING, GRAMMAR AND VOCABULARY KNOWLEDGE

In this chapter we have, thus far, explored ways to improve and expand knowledge and use of vocabulary, spelling, punctuation and grammar. In this activity we will consider how to combine, consolidate and test out all of these skills with a text. In other words, we will see how thoroughly and competently the pupils can **edit** a text, with all that that encompasses.

METHOD

> Share the following flashback story about the origin of Emerald Soldier Jack Jordan with the pupils:

jack jordan was in the middle of a dead bad war with sum nasty alien thingies. he stopd for a bit to luck at his ring. He started too fink about wear he had got it.

5 years earlier, jack he had wokened up hearing voices telling him two drive to the beach when he got their he seen a really upset dying alien what gave a him a ring and told him he had been chosen 2 be a cosmic soldier whose job it was to save the world.

a bang mayed Jack wake up from this daydream. He got ready to finished the fight. He felt good and tough.

> Clearly, as in the last example, this is a text with many errors. However on this occasion, instead of simply correcting the text, ask your class to edit it. This, of course, involves using their spelling, punctuation and grammar skills to correct the technical errors, but it also involves using their expanded vocabulary and knowledge of effective phrase types to improve the text as they go. Challenge them to re-write the piece so that it tells the same story, but in the most engaging, exciting, accurate and skilful way as they can, using all the editing techniques they have been practising.

An edited example based on the previous text and teaching suggestions, by Kuhali, aged 9:

Jack Jordan was in the centre of a blood-splattered, vicious war with many deformed, ferocious aliens. He paused for a second to gaze at his ominous, luminous ring. He started to recall how he had got this amazing ring, and his mind whirled around like a tornado as it hunted down the memory.

A few years earlier, Jack was woken by ghastly voices haunting him, telling him to go and travel to the beach. When he arrived there he spotted a dying alien, groaning and moaning like a dying car engine. Wounded and hurt, dying and injured, the alien moaned for Jack to come to him. Slowly, it handed him a mysterious ring. It was glowing like a creature's eyes in the dead of night. The alien spoke to him, it groaned to him that his job was to save the world, then it died.

A deafening bang awoke Jack from his day dream. He started up like a race car and got ready to save the world from perishing...

> As an extension of this task, provide the pupils with a badly written story which is appropriate to the genre you are studying, but with fewer obvious errors than the previous piece. For example:

EmCl   AdLi   SpVe   SpAd

The doctor came into the room. "I've got some bad news." he said. The family

ShNT

looked really sad, they already knew what he was going to say. The doctor

EmCl   Adv   AsAd

closed the door. He sat down. He opened his mouth to speak again.

You can see that certain annotations have already been made to the text. Each one is a coded hint at an edit that could be included. They relate to the following key:

EmCl = Subordinate Clause
AdLi = Adjective List
SpVe = Speaking Verb
SpAd= Speaking Adverb
ShNT= Show Not Tell
Adv = Adverb
AsAd = As Adverbial

You may, of course, decide on your own key codes, related to the terminology used in your school, and this list is not exhaustive. Once the pupils become accustomed to recognizing these hints and applying the relative editing techniques, you can use a key like this as a shorthand marking and amendment tool. In other words, instead of correcting every error in a piece of work in order to show a pupil mistakes or potential improvements (essentially editing on their behalf) you now have a quick way of suggesting edits which THEY can apply.

DEVELOPING LOCATIONAL WRITING THROUGH PERSPECTIVE SHIFTS

In this chapter we have employed a combination of dialogue and third-person narratives to improve spelling, punctuation, vocabulary and grammar skills. Now, to embed and develop those skills, we will consider first-person perspectives, with a particular focus on locational writing.

ACTIVITY 6.12: WHAT'S THE VIEW LIKE FROM OVER THERE?
SWITCHING FROM THIRD- TO FIRST-PERSON PERSPECTIVE

One of the editing skills developed in the previous section of this chapter was selecting and then embedding suitable vocabulary. We will consider how to secure this technique via the challenge of changing a third-person piece of locational writing to a first-person account.

METHOD

> Before the pupils undertake this task, clarify the difference between the two narrative perspectives. Explain that by experiencing a story through a single character's eyes (first-person perspective) we may get a biased and sometimes limited view. (This restricted view can be more personally engaging and does provide an opportunity to discover more about the character, but pupils do need to be able to accurately apply both forms.)

> To support the pupils, our initial third-person description is taken from Activity 5.6. In that activity we worked on drawing descriptive vocabulary out of character traits, which was then used to compile an omniscient description of a setting. Share the following example with the pupils:

Castle Chill towered above Starcomet as he strode through its cavernous opening. Its walls were made of crystals that pierced the air like a warrior's sword. These rocks, although icy and jagged in their appearance, felt strangely warm and smooth under his fingers. Peering up at the statue of his father, Starcomet could almost hear a warm voice welcoming him home, and the smell of clean air was a welcome change to the polluted streets of Megatropolis.

Although it was merely a statue, the towering crystal sculpture of his father made Starcomet feel protected. He spent so much time defending and caring for others that it was a relief for him to feel safe, cared for and loved. He finally felt as if he was home.

As the relief spread over him, Starcomet began to relax his heavy shoulders, painful from the strain of all his heroic feats. He removed his cape and, although it was not heavy to such a strong being, he felt immediately free of all the worries and responsibilities that came with it. He ambled up to a large crystal and looked at his reflection, something he usually only did when checking his Jonathan Steel disguise to make sure he looked nerdy enough. But the crystal reflection showed him who he really was, a protector, and it showed him that no matter how tired he got, he must be the hero people needed him to be. Finally, Castle Chill silently assured him that this place would always be there for him, his lifelong friend, his guardian and his home.

> Review and discuss the character traits which are exemplified in the text, highlighting key phrases and vocabulary. Establish the character's mood, and then explain to pupils that you are now going to try and get 'inside Starcomet's head.' Model the rewording of the first paragraph using the following example:

My home, Castle Chill, towered above me as I entered through its familiar, cavernous opening. Its walls, made of crystals, reminded me so much of my lost planet, the rocky world of Alcotron. Although some might think these rocks icy, jagged and threatening, to me they felt warm and smooth. I peered up at the statue of my father, as I always did, and I could almost hear his warm, familiar voice welcoming me back. The smell of clean air was a welcome change to the polluted streets of Megatropolis, although I already missed my adopted city.

> Draw the pupil's attention to the words in bold red type. Ask them why these words, in particular, had to be changed, eliciting the fundamental idea that the use of personal pronouns (I, my, me, his etc.) is a key feature of a first-person narrative, as they make it clear who the narrator is, as well as clarifying their relationship to other characters. Once this is understood, challenge the pupils to continue the rewrite using their editing skills. These could be sharply focused, as in the example below:

Punctuation errors:
    although it was merely a statue a crystal sculpture of his Father the towering figure made Starcomet feel protected? he spent so much time defending and caring for other's that it was a relief for him to feel safe cared for and loved! he finally felt as if he was home,

Spelling errors:
    Althow it was merely a stachoo, a crystal sculpcher of his farther, the towering figger made Star Comet feel protededed. He spent so mutch time defendin and careing for others that it was a reeleef for him too feel safe, cared for and loved. He finaly felt as if he was home.

Vocabulary and tense errors:
    Although it is merely a statue, a rock model of his father, the big figure makes Starcomet feel nice. He spent so much time being good and helping others that it is really really great for him to feel fine, happy and glad. He finally felt as if he is home.

> As an extension activity you may use the editing key developed at the end of the last section to enable pupils to employ some of the other techniques and specialist phrases they have learned, for example:

Adv

He spent so much time defending and caring for others that it was a relief for him to feel safe, cared for and loved. He finally felt like he was home.

Voc

AsAd

Using the hints from the key, this section could be edited for both perspective and vocabulary to look something like this:

I spent so much time selflessly defending and caring for others that it was a relief for me to feel secure, guarded and treasured. As I ventured further into the Fortress, I finally felt like I was home.

ACTIVITY 6.13: A WHOLE NEW OUTLOOK
USING CHARACTERISTICS TO INFORM
A FIRST-PERSON SETTING DESCRIPTION

Now we will consider how to combine the previous perspective changes with the pupils' improved editing skills in a more comprehensive way.

METHOD

> Explain that they are going to write a new first-person description of an exciting setting, one which simultaneously tells the reader about the place and reveals something about the personality of the character they choose. In terms of providing a stimulus for the setting, provide either a picture of a setting,

...or the name of a setting with a list of features, e.g.

The V.I.P.E.R Hovercarrier

• Military aircraft carrier and base, capable of flight.

• Large flight engines mounted on the side of the vessel (partially underwater.)

• 500 metre runway with jets and helicopters on top deck.

• Below deck - corridors with science labs.

• Lower deck - interrogation rooms and prison cells.

...or a short, neutral description of the setting (i.e. purely descriptive, with no emotional content) e.g.

As you board the V.I.P.E.R hovercarrier you will notice the engines mounted on each side of the vessel. These are mostly submerged when the carrier is in water and are used to propel it into the sky when flight mode is selected. The top deck of the ship features a 500 metre runway and houses a squadron of 30 jets and 15 strike helicopters. As you move inside and pass through the walkways you will see the laboratories where V.I.P.E.R scientists develop and test new weapons technology. Travelling downwards, the lower decks are used for prisoner interrogation and imprisonment.

> Decide as a group which character you would like to 'be' as you board this vessel for the first time, describing what you see as you move around. This decision will provide you with the opportunity to revisit and discuss characterisation and inferred character reactions, as the pupils will base their descriptions on how they think the character might react to their surroundings according to their personality and back story. For example, The Stellar Warrior is a soldier who might feel 'at home' on the military Helicarrier. However, he has been lost in a time warp since 1945, so he might be in awe of the modern technology on show.

> Based on the combination of your selected character's personality and the locational stimuli, brainstorm some descriptive vocabulary as a class. For example:

The Stellar Warrior might describe the Helicarrier and its parts as:

massive, astounding, shiny, submerged, new, intimidating, electrical, powerful, noisy, cramped, baffling, hi-tech, dangerous, impressive, never-ending, vast, clinical, maze, mind-blowing, dark, long, interesting, exciting, safe, confusing, miraculous, gleaming.

> Using the following example, explore and discuss the ways in which the brainstormed, character-specific vocabulary (red text) has been used to give a personal bias to the previously neutral description. At the same time, take the opportunity to secure the use of personal pronouns (green text) to establish the first person perspective:

> Based on the combination of your selected character's personality and the locational stimuli, brainstorm some descriptive vocabulary as a class. For example:

As the General leads me onboard the V.I.P.E.R hovercarrier I can't help but notice the mind-blowing, massive engines mounted to each side of the vessel. I'm new here, the 21st century is taking some getting used to, and sights like these still astound me.

"These engines are mostly submerged...when the carrier is in deep water," the General informs me as he gestures out to sea.

"Submerged!" I manage to splutter. "So how do they not flood and malfunction?" More confusing still is how they propel something this vast into the sky! As we march across the top deck of the ship, a long runway stretches out in front of us. We are surrounded by T68 fighter jets, 30 in all, backed up by 15 brand new Delta-Strike choppers. I'd love to see the enemy's faces when that bunch appears on the horizon!

We go inside, passing through a maze of clinical, confusing corridors that lead to baffling, hi-tech laboratories. I see V.I.P.E.R scientists working hard to develop and test new weapons technology, and a sharp pang shoots through me as I remember a time when I was one of those projects. We venture deeper into the never-ending ship and reach the lower decks. I see darkened, intimidating interrogation rooms, dank, cramped prison cells, and a definite increase in armed guards. It's clear to me that whoever is taken down here...stays down here.

> After exploring the text, ask the pupils to use the stimulus you have provided, along with the vocabulary you generated as a group, to create their own biased, first-person setting descriptions based on the character they have selected.

ACTIVITY 6.14: AN ALTERNATE VIEW
CREATING AN OPPOSING FIRST-PERSON DESCRIPTION OF SETTING

Not everyone sees the space they inhabit in exactly the same way. To introduce the idea that two characters might have very different perceptions of exactly the same setting, ask the pupils one or more of the following questions:

How do you think a waiter would describe a restaurant differently from the way a customer might?

How do you think a teacher would describe a classroom differently from the way a pupil might?

How do you think a doctor would describe a hospital ward differently from the way a patient might?

How do you think a professional footballer would describe a football pitch differently from the way a fan might?

(Obviously, once the pupils get the idea of these comparisons you can personalise them to appeal to the cohort.)

METHOD

> From the introductory discussion, draw out the point that, depending on the character's personality, how they view a place can be quite different from another character's perspective, even though they are in exactly the same physical space. To explore this in comic terms, stick with the same setting (in this case, the V.I.P.E.R Helicarrier) and ask the pupils to select a character who is noticeably different to the one they used in Activity 6.13. For example, if they used a character who, on the whole, was happy, impressed and excited to be on the Helicarrier (e.g. The Stellar Warrior), ask them to think of someone who might have reason to be unhappy, sceptical and perhaps even threatened by being onboard the vessel (e.g. Starcomet).

> Use the back story and personality of this new character to create a fresh set of descriptive terms for the setting. At this point you can start to draw comparisons and indentify noticeable differences in the way the two characters view their surroundings. For example:

Starcomet might describe the Helicarrier and its parts as:

Prison, stolen, cramped, clinical, intimidating, copied, small, useless, worrying, dark, confined, futile, claustrophobic, dank, trap, unnerving, long, hostile, vast, imposing, scary, surrounded.

> Again, using the example below, identify and discuss how the new, opposing vocabulary (red text) has been used to give a very different personal bias to the description. Check over the use of personal pronouns (green text) to establish the first person perspective as you go:

I follow the General at a safe distance as he leads me on to the imposing V.I.P.E.R helicarrier. It looks like a floating prison to me, all steel and locks, and I almost don't notice the vast engines mounted to each side of the vessel. FV-Hydropulse engines. I know because a good friend of mine designed them, then V.I.P.E.R stole the designs and made him disappear. They're good at that.

"Amazing design, these engines are mostly submerged when the carrier is in deep water," the General informs me, as if I didn't already know.

"Amazing!" I echo sarcastically. "I'm sure the design team had quite a job avoiding flooding." I try to sound calm, distracting myself by mentally checking over the thrust velocity calculations that propel this vast machine into the sky. As I walk reluctantly across the top deck of the ship, a long runway stretches out in front of us. I am surrounded by 30 T68 fighter jets and 15 Delta-Strike choppers, and all I can think of is how useless every single one of them would be against me.

We go inside, passing through a series of confined, clinical corridors. Each feels more claustrophobic than the last. I see V.I.P.E.R scientists, scurrying around laboratories, working on new and improved ways to blow things up. They look me up and down, and I'm sure all they see is another weapons project.

Sweating and shaking slightly, I am led deeper into the bowels of the ship. I see interrogation rooms, prison cells, and a group of armed guards who look more nervous than I am. I begin to realise that they intend to make this my new home. I don't like that idea...

> Again, after exploring this text, ask the pupils to switch to their new character and, using the same stimulus (and the new vocabulary generated as a group) create an alternative first-person description. Remind them that the more distinct the second character is, the more striking they will be able to make the differences between the two descriptions. (E.g. compared to someone like The Stellar Warrior, Thor, the Norse God of Thunder, might be intimidated and threatened by this colossal war craft. On the other hand, Magmaman, the enemy of the Z-Men, might describe his malevolent joy at spotting multiple opportunities to use his destructive magnetic powers on his surroundings).

ACTIVITY 6.15: WHERE AM I?
WRITING OPPOSING FIRST-PERSON DESCRIPTIONS FOR REAL-WORLD SETTINGS

The prompt questions from the start of the previous activity are useful for introducing the idea that two characters can have very different experiences and perceptions of the same space. They can also be used after the pupils have started to explore this concept in comic writing to bring the idea into the 'real world'.

METHOD

> Display some visual prompts for 'real world' settings, as well as introducing two characters who might have different perspectives on the same physical space:

SETTING: POLICE STATION

SETTING: ROCK CONCERT

CHARACTER 1: POLICE OFFICER

CHARACTER 2: CRIMINAL

CHARACTER 1: ROCK STAR

CHARACTER 2: GRANDMA

SETTING: MOUNTAINS

CHARACTER 1: CLIMBER

CHARACTER 2: MOUNTAIN RESCUE WORKER

> Ask the pupils to repeat the same process they applied using comic-based examples, generating vocabulary ideas that are specific to the 'character' and combining them with other visual information from the stimulus to create two distinct, first-person descriptions.

> When the pupils are confidently applying the narrative techniques to the real world stimuli, expand the activity further by providing only the setting and asking the pupils to think of two characters who would look at the space differently. Then, using them as part of the process they have learned, compile two opposing descriptions.

> Finally, remove all the stimuli and scaffolding. Ask pupils to generate their own setting, then think of two differing characters who might inhabit the space. They will then follow the established steps to create two different descriptions. They can also consider how to include techniques learned throughout this chapter.

The pupils will now be able to use their developed editing techniques, encompassing improved spelling, punctuation, vocabulary and grammar skills, to craft exciting, 'real world' third- and first-person descriptions of settings and action. These may very well include accurate, engaging dialogue, and their writing will be informed throughout by their characters' personalities.

CHAPTER 7
USING COMICS TO EXPLORE COMPLEX NARRATIVE THEMES

PREFACE

Thus far, the aim of this book has been to enable teachers, through the medium of comics, to improve a variety of narrative writing skills across their whole class or with smaller groups. The intention of this final chapter, however, is somewhat different. It has been designed to encourage more able pupils to develop a deeper knowledge and understanding of more complex topics. It will open up new, cross-curricular areas of study through more demanding source material and thus facilitate increased higher-level thinking. Subsequently, not everything that follows will be suitable for all children. Some content might be particularly useful for Gifted and Talented children as a means to extend their critical and creative thinking, whilst other parts may suit the older pupil who is working to engage with more mature subject matter. As long as appropriate professional discretion is used, it is likely that both you and the pupils you work with will gain much from the following activities.

COMICS AS A RESPONSE TO HISTORICAL EVENTS AND SOCIETAL CONCERNS

Wednesday 23rd May, 2012. Comic book fans all over the world open up the new *Astonishing X-Men #50* issue to find Northstar, a mutant hero with Supermanesque powers, proposing to his long-term partner. His long-term **male** partner, Kyle Jinadu.

Cue outrage from conservative groups such as *One Million Moms*: "These companies are heavily influencing our youth by using children's superheroes to desensitize and brainwash them into thinking that a gay lifestyle choice is normal and desirable." On the other hand, the Scottish Parliament tabled a motion stating: "This Parliament welcomes the news that the Marvel comic, *X-Men*, will feature its first same-sex marriage;...it...agrees that same-sex marriage should not be restricted to the world of literature and fantasy."

At a time when same-sex marriage is becoming more widely legalised in America, supported publicly for the first time by its President, and in the U.K the Government Equalities Office is holding a public consultation on same-sex marriage, we see comics doing what they have always done extremely well. As Axel Alonso, Marvel Comics Editor-in-chief, said: "Our comics are always best when they respond to and reflect developments in the real world. We've been doing that for decades, and [the marriage] is just the latest expression of that."

As well as 'serious' topics, comics also draw from prevalent 'hot' topics and fashionable subjects. For example, Image Comics released a series called *America's Got Powers*, written by broadcaster and comic writer, Jonathan Ross, which explores the transient and often troubled nature of the instantaneous fame faced by those who appear on TV talent shows.

These examples show how comic worlds and content are not always the constructs of unrealistic visions or creative fantasy. Due to regularity of publication and the creativity of their writers and artists, they can be both current and socially relevant. This in turn provides us with an accessible vehicle through which to explore some of these societal issues in the classroom. Of course, not every comic has become explicitly concerned with gritty satire and social commentary. There is still ample opportunity to be removed from reality if one so desires (simply pick up an issue of *Green Lantern* to be whisked away to wonderful alien worlds). However, whether it be contemporary social commentary, reflections upon recent history, or even timeless Greek or Norse tales told through graphic form, the comic can offer the reader, and the teacher, an accessible 'way in' to some extremely complex issues and ideas.

ACTIVITY 7.1: A HERO FOR A NATION
CREATING WAR PROPAGANDA

Steve Rogers, a.k.a. Captain America, was a genetically enhanced super soldier, the result of a fictional collaboration between American and German scientists during World War Two. What you might not know is that the character of Captain America was a purposefully political creation, a reaction by *Timely Comics* writers, Joe Simon and Jack Kirby, to the atrocities being committed by Nazi forces at that time. In other words, the creation of Captain America was yet another example of comic writers harnessing social concerns and translating them into a graphic narrative. When that narrative, entitled *Captain America Comics #1* was released in December 1940 in the midst of World War Two, it sold over one million copies. The cover depicted the eponymous hero 'socking Adolf in the jaw' (...as he would put it).

The fact that early issues of this comic went on to outsell copies of publications such as *Time* magazine might distract us from the point that this publication was created to be more than a comic. In reality, it was full-on war propaganda, and that is where it becomes most useful and interesting to us as teachers.

> Show the pupils the cover of *Captain America Comics #1* (unable to reproduce here due to copyright – Google keywords '**Captain America #1**') and use it to introduce the idea of war propaganda. Agree a definition of the term that includes the idea of information produced by a certain military group to promote their own specific 'ends', often at the expense of the beliefs of others. In terms of striking this contrast, look together at some examples of graphic propaganda from other countries involved in World War Two:

Nazi cartoon from a magazine published 1941-1942 in Germany depicting Jews as responsible for world political upheaval.

British WW2 propaganda promoting conversational discretion.

Search engine keywords:
WW2, British, German, Nazi, Jewish, Propaganda, Poster, Comic, Cartoon

Discuss how these posters work, the messages they convey, the stereotypes they use and their intended effect. Debate whether the style of their presentation (i.e. the use of comic illustrations) lessens their seriousness and impact, or perhaps helps to make it 'acceptable' to spread messages of hate and violence.

> Using the opinions and observation garnered from the scrutiny of the propaganda pieces, ask the pupils to imagine themselves as British comic writers in 1940. How might they employ a similar graphic style and technique to create a WW2 propaganda poster to introduce their own fictional national icon: 'Major Britannia'?

> Ask the pupils to include a tag line for their new military hero based on the rhetoric they picked up when analysing the propaganda pieces e.g.

A Man of the Flag,
a Man for Britain.

Major Britannia,
leading the war for
freedom!

He enlisted,
he fights,
and he will win.
Fascists beware!

> Once the pupils have established their character, ask them to use the storyboard planner from Chapter 3, to plan their own eight-frame origin story for their hero. Using this, ask the group to create the first issue of *Major Britannia Comics*, (in comic form) as well as the first serialised *written* story chapter for newspaper publication.

> As an extension and cross-curricular link to Design Technology and Art, you could ask the pupils to create promotional packaging for the first issue of the comic, including appropriate token giveaway gifts. Ask the pupils to research/mind map possible 1940s children's toys and use their findings to design and produce suitable gifts. These could include a set of playing cards, stickers, a small military toy, badges, a folding paper Spitfire plane, or any other ideas you/they deem appropriate.

ACTIVITY 7.2: THIS ALL SEEMS A BIT FAMILIAR
EXPLORING VICTORIAN FEARS IN LITERATURE

The practice of drawing on societal concerns to inspire fantastical literature stretches back into literary history long before World War Two. One particular period in which it seemed rife, and which spawned characters so memorable that they have since been adopted by modern comics, is the Victorian age. Take, for example, *The Strange Case of Dr Jekyll and Mr Hyde* by Robert Louis Stevenson. Here is a cautionary tale about an overreaching scientific endeavour that lacked any consideration of the potentially disastrous results. It was also an exposé of the Victorian paradox between outward respectability and inward animalism. Sound familiar...?

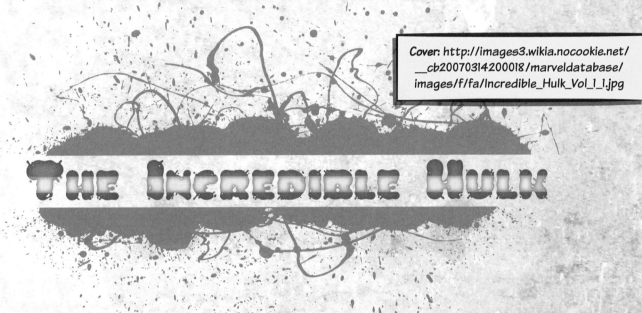

Cover: http://images3.wikia.nocookie.net/__cb20070314200018/marveldatabase/images/f/fa/Incredible_Hulk_Vol_1_1.jpg

Or perhaps that same theme of the duality of man, combined by Bram Stoker with other prominent Victorian concerns regarding immigration, technological advancement and interracial relations, could inspire a half-breed, vampiric anti-hero who would go on to be the star of a Hollywood trilogy..?

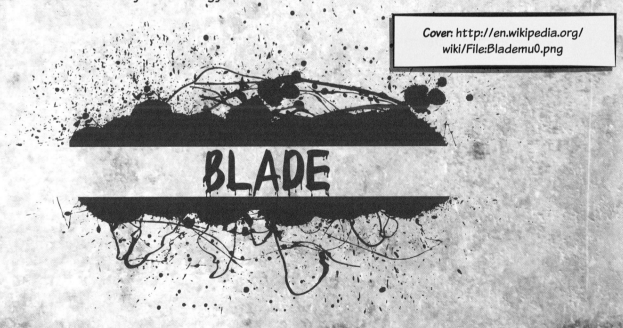

Cover: http://en.wikipedia.org/wiki/File:Blademu0.png

Maybe a character who embodied concerns regarding scientific enhancement (which some Victorians believed to be tampering with the work of God) and who featured in what was arguably the first science fiction novel could reappear in exactly the same form in modern comics. A reminder, perhaps, that in the 21st century we still share concerns about the consequences of invasive scientific advances...?

> Using your professional discretion, select from and discuss the above examples, showing how older literature, like modern comics, used the concerns and fears of the society of the time to create characters which would engage readers. Discuss how the protagonists would either embody (Frankenstein's monster) or oppose (Dr Jekyll) the very issues that were foremost in the reader's mind.

> Ask the pupils to research the Victorian era with a view to discovering more about the society, and in particular, what their biggest concerns were. If they need supporting in this you might ask them to consider:

- post-colonialism
- immigration
- advances in science and technology
- the place of women in society
- the importance of social respectability
- child labour
- science as a challenge to received religious doctrines.

> Using the information garnered from their research, ask the pupils to follow in the footsteps of the Victorian authors, and the modern comic book writers, to create the back story for a new character that either embodies or opposes their focal concern. They can use the same planning resources as in the previous activity. Suggest that it might even be possible to combine concerns. Use the following example to demonstrate and discuss how a combination of concerns has been used to create an engaging character and narrative with an historical setting:

Chosen concern(s): The importance of social respectability / advances in science and technology

To embody or oppose?
My character will **embody** this concern.

The Story of Archer Harrington

Archer threw the dead body into the tall, steel cage without a second thought, knowing that the beast would instinctively follow. It took a little longer for the creature to react than he had expected, and the delay worried him more than the fact that it had escaped in the first place. However, it was soon back in its place, and Archer locked the heavy door behind it. The sickening crunching of bones and the drip, drip, drip of fresh blood was, morbidly, music to Archer's ears. It meant the struggle was over, if only for another week. Wearily, Archer surveyed the damage to his father's basement. Lots of equipment had been overturned, a small fire blazed where candle oil had spilled from a broken lamp, but nothing too dramatic. It was his own fault for forgetting the safety catch on the cage. He knew that. Still, relieved and satisfied, weary yet determined, Archer extinguished the flame and made his way back up the steep basement steps, not noticing the vial missing from the top shelf of his chemical cabinet.

"A truly delightful soirée as always, Archer!" announced a stiff, high-pitched voice as Archer Harrington rejoined his own party.
"Many thanks. Your presence is, as always, most warmly received, Madam Tenderlore," replied Archer, concealing his concern behind his usual aristocratic facade. He then proceeded to mingle with his guests, exchanging pleasantries and witticisms with his male companions, and passing smooth-tongued compliments to the ladies in attendance. No one had the faintest idea that only minutes previously, he had fed a poor, homeless girl's corpse to a bloodthirsty fiend. No one suspected a thing. No one except a curious young kitchen servant by the name of Billy Chester, who had noticed a strange smell radiating from the back grid that led to the basement furnace.

Riches, status, luxuries, these are the things to which Archer Harrington had always been accustomed. As a young boy he had watched his family's industrial empire grow; it seemed there was barely any business or production process that Edgar Harrington, Archer's father, was not a part of. The genesis of all of this, however, was Oscar Harrington, Archer's grandfather. He was a leader in industry in his own time, and was the reason that the Harrington name had long since been synonymous with wealth and leadership. In spite of this, at the age of fifty, Oscar became quite ill. In fact, Archer couldn't remember a time when he had seen his grandfather in good health. He had watched his father bring in medical experts from all over the world, all of whom claimed to have the latest cure, and none of whom made the slightest difference. One memory stuck particularly vividly in Archer's mind, the moment when the penultimate medical professional admitted defeat and told his father that there was nothing more that he, or anyone else, could do. Oscar Harrington, the giant of industry, was going to die.

A last will and testament had long since been drawn up, and Oscar's affairs were all put in order. Edgar had arranged for the local priest to perform the last rites as he sensed the end was near. That night, when a loud knock emanated from the front door, Edgar trudged reluctantly to welcome the priest. But it was not the priest who greeted him. It was a small, strange-looking man in a long, rain-sodden overcoat, pulling a large wooden cart behind him.

"Mr Harrington, I presume?" said the man in a thick, eastern-European accent.

"Why yes, and who do I have the pleasure of addressing?"

"My name is Doctor Gustav von Braggen. You contacted me regarding the ill health of your father, I hope I am not too late."

"Unfortunately sir, I believe you are. All the other physicians predict that my father will depart from our world this very night."

"Perfect timing." the doctor announced, as he dragged his cart into the hall. He proceeded to describe how he would need four strong men to install some of his equipment - 'electrodes', as he called them - on the highest points of Harrington Hall. This being completed, he had wires run down to an operating table which he set up in the basement. After completing all his preparations, he ordered that Oscar Harrington be brought down. Orders were followed, and soon Oscar lay upon the operating table, strapped in place, with wires coiled around his pale limbs.

"This is all most unorthodox," complained Edgar. "What do we do now?"

"Now, sir, we wait," replied the doctor intensely.

"Wait for what?" Edgar enquired.

"The death of Oscar Harrington."

What followed would be etched into Archer Harrington's mind for the rest of his life. He saw his father fly into a fit of rage at this supposed doctor's absurd suggestion. He saw the doctor calm his father, and explain that only at the moment of death would his reinvigorating treatment work. He saw his father accept this theory reluctantly, knowing that he really had no other choice. Finally, he saw the moment that life slipped from his grandfather's eyes.

"Now! Turn the handle! Turn on the machine!" screeched the doctor, suddenly animated and energised. A handle was turned, and the body of Oscar Harrington jumped into life, writhing and contorting, threatening to break the bonds that held him. "Off!" yelled the doctor, and the electricity died as quickly as it had commenced, and the body returned to its peaceful state. The doctor checked, and checked again; no signs of life. He was thrown out of the house soon after, followed by curses from Edgar for putting his family through that awful spectacle. They drowned out the doctor's protests, even those regarding the part of the treatment that still needed to be performed, before something terrible happened.

"What vintage is this brandy, Archer? It is absolutely exquisite!" Lord Farthenstow was almost beside himself.

"Ah that would be telling. You just enjoy it!" Archer replied as he continued to work his way through the guests at his party. He was now the CEO of Harrington Industries, following his father's mysterious disappearance five years ago, and he had a reputation to uphold, a name to live up to, and powerful allies to keep happy. Avoiding scandal had been hard work when his father had vanished. Archer had to ensure that all the right people were paid off, some to remain loyal business partners, some to write the correct things in the newspaper, and some simply to keep their mouths shut. Archer knew it was money well spent - reputation meant everything. If your name was ruined, you were ruined; it was as simple as that. Archer did what he had to do. He always did what he had to do.

Just as he was about to engage in conversation with Henry Waddock, an extremely influential politician, Archer felt a tap on the shoulder. It was his manservant, Reginald, and he looked even more pale and flummoxed than usual.

"Sorry to disturb you, sir, I most truly am, but there's been an emergency, sir."

"What the devil is going on, man?" replied Archer hurriedly, eager to return to his guests.

"I think, sir, it might be best, if you'll pardon me saying so, sir, that I tell you in...private."

"I can't leave the guests, Reginald. It's bad form. Now out with it! What's the matter?"

"Well sir, it's just that, er..." Reginald hesitated. "It's young Billy Chester, sir. They've found him out the back, near the basement grid, sir. Well, at least some of him is there, sir."

Archer's face drained to the same pale shade as his servant's. Turning quickly, he hurried to the basement door. He took out the only key, which hung on a chain around his neck, opened the door, passed through, locked it behind him and descended the stairs. What he saw shocked him; everything was exactly as it was when he had left. The only thing missing was the beast. Archer approached the cage cautiously, it was still locked. Breathing heavily, he ventured inside, everything still seemed normal. That was until he walked into the darkest, furthest recess of the cell, where he almost fell down a large hole in the floor. Impossible, he thought. The cage had been built into the ground. Even if one were to dig a hole, one would eventually reach impenetrable metal bars. It made no sense. Archer could not brave a descent down the hole, and instead clambered back into the room. As his eyes scanned for some clue or another, they came to rest on the gap on his chemical shelf. He checked off the bottles in his head, and only one was missing. Sulphuric acid. In an instant he remembered the delay in the beast's pursuit of its next meal. It had tricked him, used the distraction of the chaos it was causing to take the one thing in the basement that could eat through the bars of its cage. Oscar Harrington, the former giant of industry, now the living dead, bloodthirsty beast of Harrington Hall, was free. Archer Harrington knew what he had to do...and he always did what he had to do.

> To extend this activity further, ask the pupils to create another Victorian-inspired character to oppose their primary character in the next chapter. This time, challenge them to draw from different influences, perhaps ones that are not necessarily tied to their focal societal concern. For example, the DC supervillain Solomon Grundy, whilst reminiscent of Frankenstein's monster, was actually named after the eponymous character from a simple Victorian nursery rhyme:

Solomon Grundy,

Born on a Monday,

Christened on Tuesday,

Married on Wednesday,

Took ill on Thursday,

Grew worse on Friday,

Died on Saturday,

Buried on Sunday.

That was the end,

Of Solomon Grundy.

ACTIVITY 7.3: TALES OF GLORY!
TEACHING ANCIENT HISTORY THROUGH COMICS

In the previous activity we explored the comic practice of drawing on the concerns of bygone eras in order to inspire new characters and narratives. The source material is not, however, limited to the last century or two, nor even to the last millennium. Comic writers have used a number of mythical characters, as well as real historical figures, from thousands of years of history, and integrated them into modern comics.

An effective example of this is Thor, the Norse God of Thunder, who has appeared in Marvel Comics since 1962. His origins are the same (son of Odin and citizen of the Viking realm of Asgard). His weapon is the same (the mountain-crushing hammer 'Mjollnir'). His mythical reputation also stays intact (petulant, headstrong and fiery in his disposition). Due to this level of authenticity, the Thor comics are a fantastic tool for hooking children into Viking topic work. Furthermore, the advent of comic films, including a Thor movie, provides us as teachers with stunning visuals that present the worlds and mythical environments that we are teaching about in incredibly engaging, yet simultaneously credible, detail. We can easily show pupils the heavenly Viking realm of Asgard, the Bifrost (or Rainbow Bridge) that links the realms of Yggdrasil (the World Tree), Jotunheim (the realm of the frost giants) and even the great Gladsheim Hall in Asgard, in spectacular fashion.

This example, along with others such as Frank Miller's 300 (a graphic retelling of the Greek Battle of Thermopylae, aimed at a slightly more mature audience), demonstrates that stories from the distant past can be retold through the comic medium, making them engaging, dynamic and accessible where they might otherwise have been perceived to be old, stale and esoteric. This is a process which can be repeated in the classroom to encourage pupils to think the same way.

> Show, with the appropriate permissions (ask school administrators for video copyright forms), and your own professional discretion, the start of the 2011 film 'Thor.' Use it to engage the pupils in a discussion regarding Norse mythology which will help them to understand some fundamental aspects of Norse beliefs. Next, select a written Norse myth (collected, child-friendly editions are widely available from online bookstores) and share it with the group (or, if you are studying the Greeks, perhaps show selected, age-appropriate, clips from the promotional material for 300, then share your chosen Greek tale).

> Using the examples discussed at the start of this activity (Thor and the Spartans), explain that it is not uncommon for modern comic writers to take characters from long ago and adopt them for their new, contemporary stories. Discuss and infer possible reasons for this...

o They are heroic tales of bravery, so people still look up to the characters.

o They are characters who embody a certain moral message which still applies today.

o To show that older stories can be reinvigorated by the comic medium.

Tell the pupils that they are going to undertake the same task, attempting to reinvigorate a story from the past using the comic medium.

> Once you have a sense that the pupils are comfortable with the selected story and its content and structure, ask them to rewrite the story themselves. However, tell them that they are only able to use 12 sentences, and each sentence must not contain more than one 'event.' – Do not tell them why they are being constrained in this way. Use the following example, written for the Norse myth, 'Thor's Lost Hammer', if necessary:

1. Thor awoke one morning to find his mighty hammer Mjollnir had gone missing.

2. He searched everywhere and asked everyone, but he could not find it.

3. Loki, Thor's brother, set off disguised as a falcon to Jotunheim.

4. There, Loki discovered that Thrym, the king of Jotunheim, had stolen Thor's hammer.

5. Thrym demanded the Goddess Freya's hand in marriage in return for the hammer.

6. Loki and Thor asked Freya to do them this favour, but she refused.

7. Heimdall (the guardian of the Bifrost) came up with a plan for the brothers to disguise themselves as Freya and her handmaiden.

8. The brothers, dressed reluctantly as bride and handmaid, travelled to Jotunheim.

9. They attended the wedding feast where Thor spent all night resisting Thrym's advances.

10. Thrym eventually brought out Mjollnir as a gift to his 'bride'.

11. At the sight of his weapon, unable to bear it any longer, Thor ripped off his disguise and seized Mjollnir.

12. Thor laid waste to all of the giants in attendance, starting with Thrym.

> Once the 12-sentence stories are completed, provide the pupils with a horizontally folded A4 piece of paper where each 'page' has been split into three cells. Award team points to the pupil who can explain why the 12-sentence constraint was necessary (i.e. each sentence represents a single cell in the comic, and within each cell only one action can be illustrated, hence the limits placed on their written narrative). Have the pupils convert their 12-sentence story into a 12-cell comic, thus reinvigorating an old tale using a well-planned, modern graphic format.

> As a cross-curricular extension activity, you might consider other media that could be used to produce a similar reinvigorating effect, and at the same time provide the class with extended writing opportunities. For example, you could ask the class to convert a story into a script:

Setting: The fields of Asgard.

Thor: (furiously) Loki! Have you stolen my hammer?

Loki: (shocked) I wouldn't dream of it! But I will help you look!

(Loki leaves to find Freya, the Godess of Beauty)

Loki: (politely) Freya, you look lovely today, may I ask a favour?

Freya: (suspiciously) If you must!

Script extract for 'Thor's Lost Hammer' animation project, Jessica, aged 9.

> Subsequently, using a combination of ICT and Design Technology, ask the pupils to team up to create sets and models which they can combine with their script and ICT recording media (e.g. DigiSmart cameras) to create animated versions of the tale, using new media to reinvigorate classic stories.

The heavenly realm of Asgard

The frozen wasteland of Jotunheim

As imagined by Class 8
St Richard's RC Primary School

ACTIVITY 7.4: IT'S ALL POLITICS
USING COMICS TO CREATE A PERSUASIVE POLITICAL SPEECH

At the start of this chapter we explored the tendency amongst comic writers to draw on current societal concerns to inspire stories, with the then contemporary manifestation of this being the same-sex marriage storyline created by Marvel Comics. There has, however, been a DC Comics character who, since the 1940s, has been the personification of not just one, but a whole selection of societal fears, changing as one takes over from another. This character is Superman's arch-nemesis, Lex Luthor.

In April 1940, Lex Luthor appeared for the first time in *Action Comics #23* as a corrupt scientist whose technical knowledge and intellect were matched only by his lust for power. This was in the midst of World War Two, the time of the Manhattan Project, when the issue of scientific advances in weapons technology was at the forefront of the public consciousness. Again, we find a clear example of a character born from the concerns of the society of the time.

In the 1980s, this trend continued as Lex Luthor was re-imagined as a white-collar villain, an evil business executive who would step over anyone for the almighty dollar, and probably kick them on the way past. He was the ultimate embodiment of yuppie-era greed, the Wall Street Overlord. More recently, Lex Luthor even became President, reflecting the current societal fear of governmental intrusion and control (even coming under fire for covert arms dealing, another current 'hot topic'). A character like Lex Luthor often succeeds, as far as the hero allows him to, owing to his intellect and charm, and his ability to manipulate others. Again, this provides us with a stimulus for effective persuasive writing practice in the classroom.

> First, using the notes above, describe and discuss the changing characterisation of Lex Luthor with the group (in terms of cross-curricular links, it might be useful to work on a modern-historic timeline here to put the evolution of the character into a clear social and historical context). Subsequently, elicit ideas regarding the way his characterisation links to those we have explored in previous activities, and, based on that, ask what it is that makes Lex Luthor a 'good' villain.

> Share the following letter, addressed to another corrupt president, which contains some serious legal allegations:

Federal Bureau of Investigation
973 Pennsylvania Blv NW
Washington,
DC 25372

President Maximillion Vengeance

The White House

1600 Pennsylvania Avenue NW

Washington,

DC 20500

Dear President Vengeance,

It has been brought to my attention that you have been acting unlawfully during your tenure as President. You are hereby accused of the following unlawful activities:

1.   Evidence suggests that you have facilitated the stockpiling of private military weapons produced by a sub-company of one of your own previous businesses, a business that was supposed to have been declared bankrupt and shut down six months ago.

2.   Financial records show that six members of your council have been siphoning money from government funds, including taxpayers' money, to finance their own private projects.

3.   Since your term in office began, three of your previous business partners, who were jailed for perverting the course of justice, have had their sentences radically shortened and are now free men. Witnesses are willing to testify that the judge who decided upon this reduction in term was paid off by associates within your own team.

Subsequent to these allegations, I have no choice but to remand you into custody for questioning. The FBI has already made a public announcement, and you will have the chance to address the nation tomorrow at noon before you are brought in for questioning.

Sincerely,

FBI Director Roger T. Bueller, II

> Tell the pupils that they are now Maximillion Vengeance, the confident, charming intellectual who can talk himself out of any situation. They must write a speech, to be delivered to the world's media the next day (a possible class drama activity – pupils as paparazzi / reporters / protestors / supporters) to liberate himself from the damning charges. If necessary, support them by providing the following starter:

From the desk of President Maximillion Vengeance

People of the Great United States, and friends all over the world, I stand before you today not to answer the corrupt, unjustified charges brought against me by the FBI, nor to speak to those members of the media who would see me jailed for actions that were not my own. I stand before you, the people, to earn back what I see as truly the most precious thing to me, your trust...

At this point the pupils will be combining all they know about the use and manipulation of societal concerns, garnered throughout the work in this chapter, to create a persuasive text that presents the inverse of those concerns, a political placebo of complete fabrication. Just hope that none of them goes on to a career in politics!

USING COMICS TO EXPLORE COMPLEX SOCIAL THEMES

In the first section of this chapter we explored and harnessed the literary tendency, prevalent amongst comic writers, to draw on societal concerns in order to inspire storylines and characterisations. In this section we will continue in this direction to see how comics present and provide us with different perspectives on a whole range of more personal, humane concerns, many of which will touch almost everyone at some point. For example, we have already looked briefly at the issue of gender rights, but what about issues as widespread and damaging as bullying, racism, crime & punishment, adolescent struggles and concerns about the future? These are complicated issues which we as teachers have a responsibility to address in the classroom. Yet again, comics can provide us with an engaging means of access!

ACTIVITY 7.5: CRIME AND PUNISHMENT
DEBATING CRIMINAL AND MORAL PRINCIPLES

As was suggested in Chapter 4, "comics are sometimes perceived to be simple stories, solely concerned with the struggle between wholly *Good* guys (Superheroes) and wholly *Bad* guys (Supervillains)". As was also proposed, this simplistic, polarised view is rarely accurate. We proved this when we discovered that there were characters who had turned from 'good' to 'bad', and vice versa, and some who milled around in the moral-middle. In this activity though, we are actually going to consider characters who are generally agreed to be 'good' guys, as we (hopefully) see ourselves to be, but who all, surprisingly, have radically different views on that which they seek to eradicate or enforce. This analysis will lead us to the following question: if we as people are all 'good,' does that mean we should all share the same beliefs on the nature of crime and appropriate punishments? Or do comics, as we might suspect, mirror the world around them and therefore demonstrate a variety of moral viewpoints?

> Present the class with the following three character profiles:

Name: The Enforcer
Area of operation: Slum City
Occupation: Police officer, Government Enforcement Agency
Notes: The Enforcer graduated second in class from the Academy of Law and quickly ascended the police ranks. He is the most well-renowned officer of his time, having saved his city on multiple occasions. His commitment to serving and protecting the community is unquestionable.

Name: DarkSpectre
Area of operation: Eagle City
Occupation: CEO of Symposium Research
Notes: After helping to raise his two younger siblings following the death of his parent in a car crash, DarkSpectre uses his vast wealth to fight crime and corruption in his city and around the world. He has no special powers, but has dedicated his life to helping others and watching over the people of Eagle City.

Name: Starcomet
Area of operation: Megatropolis
Occupation: Writer
Notes: Sent to Earth as research project by an alien race, Starcomet was raised in a family of four in Alabama, America. As he grew up, he assumed the role of protector of Earth, the planet that had cared for him when he most needed it. He is compassionate, honest and will never give up.

> Ask the pupils to decide whether these characters are 'good' or 'bad' guys. The answer may seem obvious, but encourage them to justify their opinions as to what makes their chosen character 'good,' thereby generating a picture of the moral qualities that the group holds in high esteem (i.e. "Starcomet, because he saves the most people", or "The Enforcer, because his only job is protecting his community"). Extend this discussion by asking which character the pupils think represents 'the greatest good' (in other words, which character do the pupils see as doing the most 'good', according to their own definition of the concept. To some, bravery might be good, to others, the ability to save the greatest number of lives might equate to the 'greatest good'). Ask them to include comparisons to back up their opinions. You might prompt them by giving your own example, e.g.

I think DarkSpectre represents 'the greatest good' because he has no special powers or healing abilities, nor does he have the support of a team of law enforcers around him. He works alone, using his own money and risking his own life, and that makes him extremely brave and selfless.

> Once the moral viewpoint of the group regarding these characters is established, provide them with the following, modified character profiles:

Name: The Enforcer
Area of operation: Slum City
Occupation: Police officer, Government Enforcement Agency
Notes: The Enforcer has the right, bestowed by law, to act as judge, jury and, if necessary, executioner. This means he is allowed, with no witnesses or support needed, to sentence a criminal to death, and kill them. He has done this over 100 times.

Name: DarkSpectre
Area of operation: Eagle City
Occupation: CEO of Symposium Research
Notes: DarkSpectre has a strict code against killing criminals, no matter what they have done. However, he is a master of multiple forms of martial arts and weaponry, and he will not hesitate to torture criminals, break bones and leave lasting physical damage to get the information he needs.

Name: Starcomet
Area of operation: Megatropolis
Occupation: Writer
Notes: Starcomet is so concerned about human life that he has previously caught bullets that have bounced off him to stop them hitting innocent bystanders. He tries to cause as little harm as he can to criminals, and makes handing them over to the proper authorities his top priority.

> Again, ask the pupils to decide whether these characters are 'good' or 'bad' guys. Has the extra information changed the answer to what might have previously been considered an 'easy' question? Whether or not they have changed their minds, have them provide specific reasons for their decision using the new information. This will allow you to elaborate on the moral qualities that the group considers important. Extend this discussion by asking how each character's treatment of human life affects how 'good' we perceive them to be and, subsequently, who do they now think represents 'the greatest good'? You might decide to challenge them by giving an unexpected opinion, e.g.

I think The Enforcer represents 'the greatest good' because he works inside the law, and the law states that some criminals do such terrible things that they must be punished by death, a punishment that DarkSpectre and Starcomet cannot ensure takes place.

> This discussion could lead the group into further analysis and examination of real world authority figures; the roles and responsibilities of law enforcement; the use of force by police, and the pupils' opinions of extreme measures of punishment (e.g. do they think it is ever right to condemn someone to life imprisonment, or to death?). You could ask them, if appropriate, to write and present a debate based on these issues, or the differences between the moral standpoints of the comic characters they have looked at versus their own. They could also research some real world vigilantes (e.g. Seattle people's hero, Phoenix Jones) and decide whether the shift from comic pages into their own reality might change their view on moral 'good'. At the end, draw the group back to the question that started this line of enquiry – "If we as people are all 'good,' does that mean we should all share the same beliefs on the nature of crime and appropriate punishments?" Hopefully the pupils will, through their own research and critical thinking, have come to a point where one thing they can agree on is that moral stances can vary dramatically from person to person. This is arguably why the most interesting crime and punishment narratives are those that deal with the moral grey area between seemingly obvious 'right' and seemingly obvious 'wrong.'

> In terms of extending this discussion, perhaps in a cross-curricular theological direction, you can again find interesting, accessible stimuli in comics. Images such as the one underneath can present spirituality, and the idea of finding balance between justice and punishment in the context of an afterlife, in unique and intriguing ways:

> This visual metaphor for the judgement of one's life could lead to additional debate and narrative work. For instance, you could recreate the balance on a display, place an unnamed character somewhere on the line, then ask the pupils to infer their back-story, including what happened to them and what they did to deserve that specific place on the balance. In terms of a religious discussion, you might ask whether this is how they imagine (imagine, not 'believe') the idea of 'eternal judgement' to be, or could they come up with their own visual metaphor (e.g. an accounting-style ledger with 'good' and 'bad' deeds totted up in columns, or perhaps a moving timeline of a life which switches from colour to black-and-white depending on the moral merit of the focal action). It will obviously be important not to suggest that any of these imaginings are 'correct', but instead the focus should be on how we can think about and represent morality and justice in expressive and engaging ways.

ACTIVITY 7.6: BULLIES, STRUGGLES AND RESPONSIBILITIES
DEALING WITH GROWING AND CHANGING

Can you imagine Spider-man being beaten up for his lunch money, or Superman being pushed around at work, and all either of them do in response is apologise and stare at the floor? Some of the toughest, most popular and well-renowned superheroes are, in alter-ego form, victims of bullying. Clark Kent, the alter-ego of the all-powerful Superman, is abused, belittled and threatened with dismissal from his job at the *Daily Planet* on a regular basis. This abusive existence is compounded for Peter Parker, aka Spider-man, who is made to suffer the responsibilities of superhero life and the adolescent struggles of an awkward, bullied teenager simultaneously.

Before Spider-man, prominent teenage characters in comics were often relegated to 'sidekicks.' (e.g. James 'Bucky' Barnes, Captain America's 15-year-old helper, or Dick Grayson, a.k.a Robin, Batman's youthful crime-fighting partner). This was, perhaps, due to the authorial assumption that the target readership could more easily imagine themselves as superhero helpers, standing next to and being protected by the hero, rather than actual superheroes. Spiderman's creators, Stan Lee and Steve Ditko, shifted that dynamic to create a nerdy, victimised, awkward teenager (who many readers could relate to) who secretly had strength, confidence and extraordinary abilities (a fantasy for any struggling adolescent reader).

Spider-man was subsequently made to fend for himself and his elderly aunt, constantly struggling to attend a part-time job to help pay rent (where, like Superman, he seems under constant threat of being fired) whilst trying to finish school (where he is relentlessly taunted and bullied, especially by arrogant jock, Flash Thompson). All of these problems, paired with the responsibility of fighting crime and continually saving his city, make Spider-man a useful character to use in the classroom. To a young person who may be struggling with growing and changing, the character is easy to relate to, thereby providing teachers with an engaging means of access to troubling personal issues such as bullying and increasing responsibilities. Spider-man is brave and heroic, facing his problems head-on, which provides us with an inspiring role-model and the means to communicate with pupils about the various pressures of growing up.

> Share the following electronic diary extracts from Strikeback's diary with the pupils:

James' ThoughtPad

Monday

Got in2 school late 2day as had 2 help Gran shift sum things down from the attic. She says she is just gettin organised, have a feelin she is looking 4 things to sell again :(- Dad's still struggling 2 find a job. Missed 1/2 of 1st class, Mrs Holbrook gave me detention. She hasn't taught me anything new since 10th grade, I'd probably do a better job of teaching that class. Max the muscle-bound moron took my lunch money as usual, had 2 stash spare change in my sock. Managed 2 get a chocolate bar without him seeing but still spent rest of day hungry. Tomorrow I'm going 2 stand up 2 him. Definitely. Probably. At least I have the science trip 2 look 4ward 2, can't w8 2 c the proton acceleration lab, v.exciting! If I can manage 2 stay away from Max + his gang I might just enjoy the whole day!

#YeahRightJames.

Tuesday

Just back from science trip + feelin v.odd. Day started well 4 once, had a gr8 morning @ the science trip. Amazing work going on with proton modification + restructurin, all right up my street! Was brill right up till lunch time wen Max + his cronies caught up with me. Ended up with that stupid meathead's protein shake poured over my head. Went 2 find a place to get cleaned up after they'd finished + managed 2 find my way in2 some kind of restricted area full of experi-mental machines. There was a section 4 protonic fusion + I was lookin inside a huge chamber wen I heard a massive bang with a flash of blinding light. Not sure what happened xactly but I legged it and made it back on the bus, haven't felt right since. Took a nap wen I got home as I felt sick + dizzy, been awake 4 a few hours. It's weird though, I feel great. As in better than ever. I feel strong, quick, powerful. I've just done 200 press ups + didn't even break a sweat! I couldn't even do 10 before! Somethin has happened 2 me. It's l8 now so I'm off 2 bed, but I hope this feeling stays!

Current Status: Excited!!! :-D

> Discuss the problems that James faces in the first entry. As a group, work to generate some possible solutions to the following issues:

- **How could James help his Nan and Dad?** (Get a part-time job / Use his computer skills to help his Dad with job websites and Nan with online shops to sell her unwanted goods / Look into support from local public services).

- **How could James deal with the teacher he doesn't get on with?** (Talk to her about his troubles at home so she can better understand his situation / Offer to do additional work or research to show his enthusiasm / Ask for more difficult work so he feels challenged again).

- **How could James deal with Max?** (Discuss the problem with a teacher, mentor or friend he trusts / Be assertive, stand up to Max and tell him no / Try to find out why Max targets him and do something about the cause of the problem).

> Read through the second entry together and discuss what might have happened differently had James followed the group's advice after the first discussion. You could use role play to act out these hypothetical situations, freezing to discuss reactions and rewinding to test out alternative ways of dealing with conflict. You could even modify the events of the day to include aspects that are of particular concern in your class/school. Extend this by thinking about the change that has come over James and what that might mean for the next day's events.

> Ask the pupils to write the next part of James's diary, covering the following day in school, including his encounters with his teacher and Max (again, these could be dramatised first to support writing). Challenge the group to explore, and strike a balance, between what James might be *tempted* to do, considering his newfound strength, and what he *should* do as a responsible, decent person.

> Finally, explain to the pupils that as James discovers more about his abilities, and subsequently realises his greater responsibilities, he decides to leave his diary behind. Ask them to write James's final entry, with a mission statement which includes the lessons he has learned, the responsibilities he is taking on, and his hopes for the future. In completing these tasks, not only will the pupils have extended and improved their diary writing based on a relatable, engaging character, but they will have worked co-operatively to suggest, discuss and evaluate a number of ways to deal with different real-world adolescent issues.

ACTIVITY 7.7: FIGHT FOR EQUAL RIGHTS
EXPLORING SOCIAL AWARENESS AND ACTIVISM

This chapter opened with an examination of the effects of a current comic storyline which featured the controversial inclusion of same-sex marriage. The comic line was from Marvel's *Astonishing X-Men*, and of all the creations in Marvel and DC comic history, there is no other group that more thoroughly represents diversity, and more emphatically campaigns for equality, than the X-Men. This effort began with their leader, Professor Xavier, a mutant with vast telepathic abilities. Upon witnessing the increasing public and governmental hostility towards mutants (who could easily be said to represent real ethnic/social/religious minorities) he established a safe haven where all were welcome without prejudice or fear. His never-failing optimism and continued efforts to build bridges and unite mutants with the rest of mankind through non-violent means have led to parallels being drawn with real-world figures such as Martin Luther King Jnr., as both championed equal rights and integration based on love, respect and a shared humanity.

Magneto, his one-time friend, now lifelong enemy, is the other side of that coin. A German-Jewish Auschwitz survivor and former inhabitant of the Warsaw Ghetto, he witnessed public and governmental hostility towards his race from the earliest years of his life. At one point he was made into a Sonderkommando, a death-camp inmate who was responsible for the disposal of the bodies of executed prisoners. After surviving the war and realising his own power (the ability to manipulate metals) he formed the Brotherhood of Mutants with the express intention that, having witnessed genocide before, he would help the emergent mutant race to defend themselves from what he saw as another oppressive threat to their civil rights, using violence if necessary. This 'by any means necessary' stance earned the character comparisons to Malcolm X, as both fought against oppression, both metaphorically and, where they believed necessary, physically.

When studying equality in school there are plenty of inspirational, influential and interesting figures to consider, (Malcolm X and Martin Luther King Jnr., as discussed, as well as people like Ruby Bridges, Mahatma Ghandi, Rosa Parks and so on). Again, without lessening the seriousness of the subject, comics give us an accessible way of introducing and engaging pupils with the topic of social and racial equality through characters with whom they are already familiar.

> Ask the pupils to carry out research based on the following question:

"Who started the X-Men and the Brotherhood of Mutants, and why?"

During their research, ask them to look for links between the characters they find, and influential figures from history they have studied. Share the results as a group and, using the findings, lead a discussion into which founder the pupils believe to be most 'righteous' in their cause and why. Hopefully, due to his anti-violence stance, they will select Professor X, in which case extend the discussion by asking them whether they can empathise with Magneto, and if so, why? (If they decide Magneto is more righteous, ask them for as many convincing reasons as possible to support their opinion and perhaps set up a debate with someone who has selected Professor X.)

> After this discussion, tell the pupils that another mutant leader has released a recorded video statement that was broadcast on television, indicting the human race for its mistreatment of mutants. He and his group have decided to fight fire with fire, and are threatening violence if certain demands are not met. These demands include, amongst other things, the automatic appointment of a mutant Prime Minister; the release of convicted criminal mutants from prison, and the establishment of a programme to limit human births so that the mutant population can grow in line with the human race. The pupils' challenge is to write and record a video reply, a persuasive presentation that uses their knowledge about his origins and world view to inform their empathetic concessions, whilst arguing the case for humanity and suggesting peaceful, sensible compromises.

> As a creative backdrop to the video message, ask the class to produce non-violent demonstration placards that include messages of tolerance and unification. Ask them to combine short but powerful language, wordplay and symbolism where possible. The result of this will be a multimedia persuasive text that demonstrates an understanding of civil rights and campaigns for it in an engaging context through imaginative, creative media.

FREEDOM AIN'T FREE, BUT WE PAY THE PRICE HAPPILY!

WE ARE ALL COLOURS OF THE SAME RAINBOW

MUTANTS' RIGHTS AREN'T WRONG, BUT WE MUST LIVE TOGETHER AS ONE!

ACTIVITY 7.8: WHAT DOES THE FUTURE HOLD?
EXPLORING DYSTOPIAN SOCIETIES

Following the analysis of individuals such as Professor X and his real-life counterparts who share positive ideologies, it might be interesting to consider a future such as the one Magneto posited in his fictional 'address to the nation': a dystopian future. A dystopia is a place where things have gone very wrong, as opposed to a utopia where all is perfect and everyone lives in harmony. Dystopian fiction is a literary genre which includes many influential works from renowned authors (e.g. *The Handmaid's Tale* by Margaret Atwood, *1984* by George Orwell, and more recently, *The Hunger Games* by Suzanne Collins). It is a genre which comic creators also enjoy exploring. Alan Moore, for example, produced *Watchmen*, an alternative, dystopian view of the late 20th century which earned a place on Time magazine's All-time 100 Greatest Novels list (note; novels, not comics), as well as *V for Vendetta*, a bleak view of a Big-Brother type society led by an oppressive and corrupt fascist government organisation known as Norsefire. Judge Dredd inhabits a dystopian future where crime is so rife that police have the responsibility to be judge, jury and executioner. Whilst these examples may not be appropriate for the majority of school pupils, they present, through the comic medium, an idea that is still incredibly interesting to consider in terms of social and behavioural studies:

"What will the future be like?"

> Using one of the following images, or one of your own that you deem appropriate for your group, present the picture with the title '100 years from now.'

> Collectively brainstorm ideas for an event that could have been the catalyst for the dystopian future you have selected (e.g. viral outbreak, alien invasion, world war, climate disaster etc). Encourage ideas that contain linked occurrences and are embellished with extra details, such as geographic location, who was involved, how people reacted, and what the short-term and long-term effects were.

> Using one of the brainstormed ideas, or one of their own if deemed suitable, ask the pupils to create a first-person recount of the catalyst. Encourage them to think about the character-specific vocabulary development work from the last chapter and challenge them to give their reader clues to the personality of their protagonist through their descriptions and reactions. If necessary you could provide story-starter prompts that give clues as to the possible nature of the narrator:

I told them this would happen. Time and again I told them, but you know what they said to me? "You're crazy, John, too many years fighting too many wars. You're just looking for trouble and you're annoyed you can't find it." Yeah, that's what they said, right until the moment the clouds parted and the first spacecraft exploded into sight...

Looking back, I can't really believe how normal the day started. I'd just dropped the kids off at school as usual, my husband James had been running late for work as usual, and I was on my way back home, listening to the radio, you guessed it, as usual. But the normally energetic, wisecracking DJ was anything but his usual self. He was reporting on an outbreak, a virus of some kind, which was having a terrible effect on people. His voice trembled as he described the infected as 'out-of-control', 'covered in boils', and at one point I thought he said 'bloodthirsty'. I wasn't sure though, as I'd been distracted by my neighbour, Mrs Adler, who was standing at my door when I pulled onto the drive. She was scratching the glass; her hands looked discoloured and scarred. Slowly, I got out of the car, and as she turned to face me I realised something was very, very wrong...

> Once the origins of the dystopia are established, challenge the pupils to switch from the first to the third-person perspective to write a description of the emergent dystopian world, including a depiction of its physical geography and its remaining society, perhaps with a focus on the progress of their protagonist from the original piece. In doing this, the pupils will be combining and consolidating much of the learning from previous chapters of this book and using it to create works of fiction that are truly imaginative and mature in their conception, and vivid and precise in their execution.

USING COMICS TO EXPLORE PSYCHOLOGY

I wonder if Captain America is feeling his age? He has, after all, been knocking around for more than 70 years. So have Green Lantern, the Joker and Batman. Spider-man, the Hulk and the Fantastic Four are all relative spring chickens... around 50 years old. These characters, along with many others in the comic world, have one thing in common; their complex identities have been built and rebuilt over many years, surviving and changing with decades of social evolution and creative embellishment. This repeated process of delving deeper and deeper into a character's persona to find what makes them tick, and if it isn't there, creating and adding it, demonstrates how comic writers and readers find the psychological *why* just as interesting as the character's actions. They want to know *why* the Joker behaves the way he does, or *why* Wolverine has such a bleak world view - what happened to them to make them that way? The process of crafting a critical event that will define and justify a character's deepest values and motivations must be as exciting to undertake as the results are to read.

This 'critical event' often differs from that which we have looked at previously, namely the 'origin story'. Origin stories can cover years of detail and contain a range of interlinked events. Now, however, we are looking specifically at the idea of a *defining moment*, where in an instant the ultimate establishing of a character's self-identity occurs. For example, Spider-man's origin story, as we discovered earlier in this chapter, includes a tough upbringing, an even tougher time at school, and an accident in a science lab. However, the 'critical event', the moment that would come to define Spider-man's core values and identity from then on, was the death of his Uncle Ben, which, due to a moment's carelessness, he indirectly facilitated. Bruce Wayne's origin story is just as lengthy, beginning with a child born into a wealthy family who becomes heir to a vast business empire and eventually dons the disguise of a giant bat to fight crime. However, the critical event within this narrative span consists merely of two gunshots in a dark alley, a moment in time that would come to define Bruce Wayne, sparking in him the drive to protect others from the same fate. Again, in *The Killing Joke*, Alan Moore presents the moment when a failed comedian and recent widower, who has been coerced into crime, flees from Batman and takes a swan dive into a vat of chemicals, emerging, insane, as the Joker. This was his 'critical event', just one moment in his life, but as he puts it, 'all it takes is one bad day to reduce the sanest man alive to lunacy. That's how far the world is away from where I am. Just one bad day.'[1]

It is within these brief, yet pivotal moments that we can witness characters discovering their true selves, and more often than not, watch them continue to wrestle with it from that day forward. For example, Bruce Wayne suffers the death of his parents and subsequently becomes Batman in order to fight criminals and deliver justice. As such, Batman comes to exist because crime exists, and he continues to exist because crime continues to exist. By the same token the Joker, in all his unhinged, anarchic glory, exists to counter Batman's ideology of law and order. These characters, like so many others in the comic world, define themselves by embodying the opposite of whatever they are in conflict with.

These crucial moments, the identities they generate, and the events which later perpetuate those identities, will be the focus of the remainder of this chapter. They will lead us to think about what defines a character, what motivates them, and how complex, psychological characterisation can inform engaging narrative writing.

[1] Moore, A. 1988. *The Killing Joke*. New York: DC Comics.

ACTIVITY 7.9: WHERE HAVE ALL THE BAD GUYS GONE?
CHALLENGING SELF-IDENTITY

Having established the idea that characters often come to define themselves by their pursuits, how can we make this fairly complex concept accessible to pupils? One way is to ask them to imagine what a character's life would be like if his or her pursuit was removed. This will enable them to recognise the importance of the tension between two characters when considering their motivation and actions.

METHOD

> Broach the topic via the following question:

Can a Superhero be a Superhero if no one causes trouble?

> Discuss the idea with the group, perhaps focusing on a selection of your collective favourite superheroes (i.e. what would The Stellar Warrior do with his time if there were no enemies left to fight? Would Jonathan Steel still need to be Starcomet? Would James Baker miss being Strikeback, or would he relish the chance to relinquish the most stressful and overbearing of his many responsibilities?).

> Ask the pupils to select the hero who they know most about and, using ideas from the group discussion, write a diary for the character's first week of 'life without villains'. Challenge the pupils to think about showing how the character may not necessarily maintain the same outlook for the whole week. If necessary, show them the following 'reaction scale':

No more criminals! I feel...

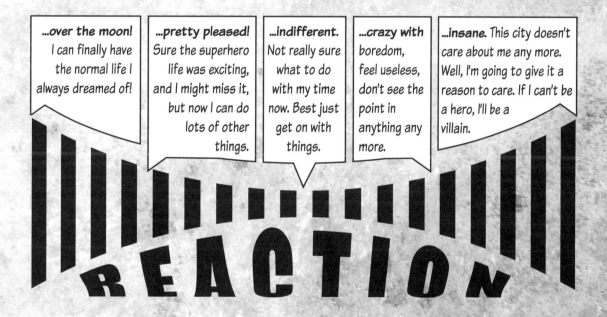

...**over the moon!** I can finally have the normal life I always dreamed of!

...**pretty pleased!** Sure the superhero life was exciting, and I might miss it, but now I can do lots of other things.

...**indifferent.** Not really sure what to do with my time now. Best just get on with things.

...**crazy with boredom,** feel useless, don't see the point in anything any more.

...**insane.** This city doesn't care about me any more. Well, I'm going to give it a reason to care. If I can't be a hero, I'll be a villain.

REACTION

Suggest that their character might start at one point on the scale, and then have an experience that shifts them to another point. Indeed, they may then have an encounter which makes them return to their original viewpoint, or to a different stance, even pushing them to an extreme on the scale.

> Extend this activity by inverting the dynamic and writing from a villain's perspective, where all the heroes have disappeared. Initially the probable consequence of this might seem obvious (mass hysteria and chaos, unchecked crime and violence). However, you could tell the pupils what happened to the Joker when he believed he had got rid of Batman. In the comic *Batman: Going Sane*, the Joker discovers that, without his nemesis to balance out his chaos and insanity, his only remaining option is to shed his Joker persona, apply for a real job, get a girlfriend and settle down as regular Gotham citizen 'Joseph Kerr'. After discussing this reaction with the class, place it on a new 'villain reaction scale' and use it to extrapolate the remaining points. The pupils can now use this as a writing prompt in the same way they did in the previous exercise.

ACTIVITY 7.10: MOOD + MORALS = ENGAGING PERSONALITY
THE MATHEMATICS OF CHARACTERISATION

In this activity we are going to consider ways to generate engaging characters by 'reverse engineering' the pivotal moments that shaped their identity. To do this, we will combine a variety of emotional states and moral standpoints using a Venn-style diagram.

> Copy and cut out the characteristic discs below. Offer them as you would a deck of cards and have a pupil pick two to start. Take their chosen discs and stick them, overlapped, on your display.

PATRIOTIC   THIEF   CYBORG   ORPHAN

ALIEN   NERD   LAW ENFORCER   UPBEAT

HONEST   INSANE   ATHLETE   SCARED

> Tell the pupils that they are going to use the selected discs to generate a new character. First, ask them, in groups, to give suggestions of the event or pivotal moment that left your character with the traits from the chosen discs. For example:

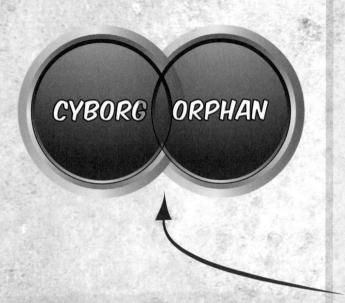

Our character was the child of two asylum seekers who, in the middle of a shelling raid in a strange country, were forced (in a **moment** of desperation) to leave their baby on the doorstep of a strange yet sturdy-looking building. Its inhabitant came out after the attack to find both parents dead but the baby unharmed. Unfortunately, the inhabitant turned out to be a renegade scientist working on modifying humans, and he raised the child not only as his son, but as his science project. The result of this was the first weaponised cyborg, codenamed Project Malice.

Our character was a shape-shifting alien and corrupt council member from the planet Narsharaa. For most of his elected term he had been defrauding the public and stealing Narshian credits. The **moment** the high council discovered his actions he was banished from his own planet and sent to live on Earth. After some time spent learning to survive, concealing himself and observing, he discovered a group of people amongst whom he knew he could hide – human politicians. Soon after, he earned a place in President Max Vengeance's government cabinet.

> Once the character-defining moment is established, ask the pupils to write a narrative which harnesses the selected characteristics and uses them to inform the character's actions and reactions. As an extension exercise you could hand out individual characteristic cards and ask the pupil to expand their story by including a new event that causes the character to take on this new trait in place of, or as well as, their existing qualities.

ACTIVITY 7.11: TURN THE ~~VOLUME~~ VILLAINY UP!
WORKING WITH CHARACTER SCALES AND TABLES

So far in this chapter we have started to use visual representations (scales and Venn-style diagrams) of characteristics and traits to demonstrate how those elements interact to shape a character's nature and inform their behaviour. We are now going to extend that to include a wider variety of combined traits, using a slightly more complex visual system.

> Share the following graphic with the group:

> Tell the pupils that between these nine vastly different characters there are actually only two variable characteristics; the degree to which the character is 'good', and the degree to which they 'uphold the law'. Check the understanding of this through quick-fire questioning, i.e., ask the pupils "Which character upholds the law but has little moral sense?" (Maximillion Vengeance). "Which character breaks the law, but has 'good' morals?" (DarkSpectre). Once this idea is understood, introduce this alternative view of characteristic interaction as 'sliding scales.'

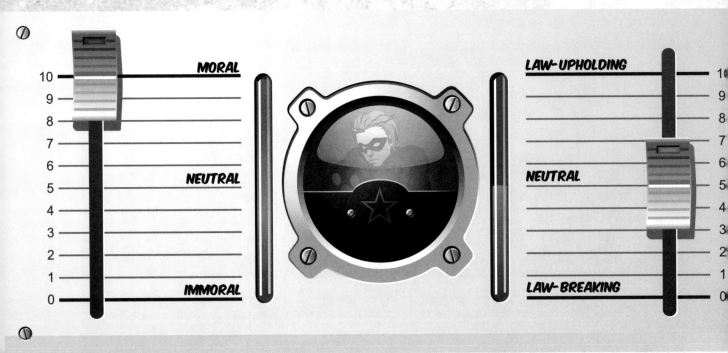

It might be useful to recreate this on a larger display or perhaps on handouts so that the pupils can grasp the concept of a sliding scale more easily. Once again, to check understanding, move stick-on sliders and ask the pupils which character embodies the displayed balance of characteristics (in this case, high moral and neutral law-breaking scores would indicate that this is the characteristic balance of Strikeback).

Once the pupils are comfortable with this visual representation it can be used to help generate new characters, much like the Venn diagram-style circles were. This time, however, the characteristics are not simply 'there' or 'not there,' but interact in a more subtle way, in that a character might have elements of a characteristic, but they could be overpowered by another, more dominant trait. For example, looking back at the table graphic, Strikeback's sense of moral good would outweigh his need to uphold the law, although not so much that he would blatantly and unthinkingly violate the rules.

> Either set the sliders for your whole group, or allow the pupils to set their own levels. Then, as in the previous activity, challenge them to generate ideas regarding the event or pivotal moment which left their character with that specific balance of characteristics. Once established, ask them to write a narrative which harnesses the selected balance of traits and uses it to inform the character's behaviour.

> You might extend this activity by introducing a third slider with a different characteristic scale to make the balance of traits even more engaging, subtle and complex. Extend further by asking the pupils to write a narrative about a character who starts with a certain balance of characteristics, then experiences an event that inverts them (not unlike the reactive scale work from the previous activity).

At this point, the pupils will be considering the balance and effect of up to three separate emotional states, using them to inform the behaviour of a psychologically intense and engaging character. Combining that with other learning from this chapter, they will be able to place these multifaceted characters in narrative contexts that reflect wide-ranging social concerns. Whether drawing from contemporary or bygone eras, addressing personal or emotional topics, they will be equipped to comment on the relevant social issues which matter to them the most.

APPENDIX 1
ALTER-EGO SCENARIOS

Use these ideas to help you write short narratives about the alter-ego you are studying.

How would your character react if...

...they were attacked by a neighbour's dog?

...they were asked to open a jam jar that no-one else had been able to open?

...they were told they couldn't leave work or they would lose their job?

...someone spilled a boiling hot drink in their lap?

...they just missed their bus?

...they saw someone in trouble but were with a friend who did not know about their double life?

...they were late for an important meeting but were stuck on a train?

...a family member wanted a birthday present that they couldn't afford?

...someone tried to mug them in a crowded public place?

...they broke something extremely valuable and precious by accident?

...their hairdresser gave them a terrible haircut?

...they were watching a film in a cinema and someone was talking loudly?

...they were playing football and the other side was cheating?

...they realised they had left their costume in the clothes bag that they had dropped off at the laundrette?

...they received a nasty letter complaining about the noise they made leaving the house late at night?

APPENDIX 2
ALTER-EGO INTERACTIONS

Use these suggestions to help you write short narratives about how an alter-ego character would react to different people in different places.

How would your character react if they met a/their...

- Teacher
- Mother
- Police Officer
- Super villain
- Best friend
- Sister
- Doctor
- Love interest
- Father
- Boss
- Brother
- A famous person

...in or at the...

Supermarket	Park	Library
Gym	Museum	Cinema
Restaurant	Airport	Bank
School	Party	Work

APPENDIX 3 – BLANK COMIC PLANNER COPYRIGHT CREATIVE EDUCATIONAL PRESS L

FURIOUS

CONFUSED

UPSET

OVERJOYED

WORRIED

CONFIDENT

GUILTY

POWERFUL

APPENDIX 5
GETTING STARTED WITH COMICS

Want to introduce comics in your classroom but not sure where to start? Here are some fantastic sources for comics to suit all needs:

Forbidden Planet – www.forbiddenplanet.com and www.forbiddenplanet.co.uk
Offering both an online shop and stores across the country, these two are great places to go for a rummage through a massive selection of old and new comics.

Travelling Man – www.travellingman.com
Another online and in-store source for comics, a particular favourite of mine due to their discount section: comics for 50p!

Silver Acre Comics – http://stores.ebay.co.uk/Silver-acre
If you are looking for specific issues, or perhaps considering collecting comics, this is the place to go!

A Place in Space – http://stores.ebay.co.uk/A-PLACE-IN-SPACE
A very reasonable online comic retailer – brand new comics with free delivery for less than ₤3.00 each!

Classical Comics – www.classicalcomics.com
Their main aim is to make classical literature appealing to all, starting with younger readers. To aid in differentiation in classes of mixed abilities, their range provides multiple text versions of each title, with the range broken down into "Shakespeare" and "Classics".

Abebooks – www.abebooks.co.uk
One of the biggest second-hand book retailers in the world – a great source for cheap graphic novels

Marvel Comics – www.marvel.com and www.marvelkids.com
An excellent source for all things Marvel, and the 'Marvel Kids' site has content aimed specifically at younger children. Marvel also has an app for mobile devices which offers free and paid comics to download.

DC Comics – www.dccomics.com and www.dccomics.com /blog/fan_family
DC's official site contains information on all DC characters, and the 'Fan Family' section has content tailored to younger children. They also have an app for mobile devices offering free and paid comics.

Comixology – www.comixology.co.uk
This site offers mainstream and independent comics to download, and also has a 'Get Schooled' section which spotlights comics that cover school age groups.

The Phoenix Comic – www.thephoenixcomic.co...
A weekly 32-page comic for children aged 8 – 12, featuring exciting story strips, a puzzle, competition and a non-fiction strip.

Megacity Comics – http://www.megacitycomics.co.uk
Another online retailer, unique in its inclusion of a school library section. Currently under development, it promises to help schools create a comprehensive comic selection.